UNVEILED

By

Kenneth M. Lee

A Marci Lane Suspense Story

Book Two

UNVEILED, by Kenneth M. Lee

ISBN 9780971185074

Copyright ©2022

Printed in the United States of America

This is a work of fiction. Names, characters, places, and incidences are purely the works of imagination, though a few of the physical locations in the Tidewater area are real. But any resemblance to actual persons, living or dead, businesses, companies, and events, are purely coincidental.

E-Mail: kenlwor@gmail.com
Blog: http://thedivineway.wordpress.com
1382 Grandpa Ln., Loris SC 29569

Kenneth Lee has self-published three other books which are available at Amazon: *God's Divine Help* (A Self-help Guide to Find Peace in God through Jesus Christ for any one of 71 subjects); *Persecuted But Not Forsaken;* and *Victim's Vengeance*

Dedication

This book is dedicated to Native Americans and
"unwitting victims" (as the C.I.A.'s MK-ultra program
documents termed them), to find truth and redemption
from the sins of the people involved in U.S. Government
programs which covertly employed human behavior
modification programs and non-consensual
experimentation upon the people.

Unveiled

Uncovering a 2000 Year Old Lie

And I saw the dead, small and great, stand before God, and the books were opened; and another book was opened; which is the book of life. And the dead were judged out of those things which were written in the books, according to their works.   *Rev. 20: 12*

1.

When James, Peter, John, and Jesus went up to the mountain that day, they had no idea that a voice from heaven would talk to them. But they had just spread God's word to the people along the shoreline.

Possibly the three disciples were looking for more in the way of religious fervor; and when a voice came out of a cloud, they were enamored, and fell on their faces in Matthew 17: 5.

They told Jesus they were going to elevate his position on earth by making a tabernacle for him.

1

But Jesus would have none of it. Not only did he tell them to disregard the vision they had seen earlier, but also the voice in The Gospel of John 12: 30.

"Now is the judgment of this world; now shall the prince of this world be cast out" (12: 31).

2200 years later, Cherokee Indian Bobby Hutchings in Virginia was not as fortunate to disregard the voice, succumbing to a voice telling him to murder a man.

But the Indians had been deceived and targeted for years, by a secret group of whites from another continent.

****

Marcia Lane sat spellbound in the courtroom in a black pants suit that she had hurriedly changed into after driving to Fredericksburg earlier in the morning to acquire some evidence for Richie Granger, her boyfriend and attorney for Bobby Hutchings, who was part Cherokee.

It wasn't the courtroom that bothered her so much. She had worked as a court reporter for years before becoming an aide and co-partner with Rufus Stronger, her boss, in the Private Investigators business.

No. She was wondering how this drama in court would play out, since it involved a sophisticated scheme and biological insertion of an implant to control a man and get him to murder someone.

Years ago, she had something similar happen – waking to find blood on her pillow and a pinprick on her ear lobe. Then, someone began stalking her electronically, and while the tenacity of it quit, she wanted justice for not only herself but also other people.

Bobby Hutchings had claimed he was being electronically stalked and coerced.

The courtroom had about twenty people in it.

A few people who sat up front looked as if they may be friends of the deceased, Presley Whitfield, who had been killed by Bobby.

An older woman and middle- aged man looked solemn with their heads bowed, and the woman shed a few tears.

Lawyers for the defendant and plaintiff sat at their respective tables in front of the judge's platform. The plaintiff was on the right side and the defendant was on the left – as one who would look out from a judge's seat.

It was a hot humid day in Henrico County, with some people fanning their faces with newspapers and others with paper foldouts, while one man waved a bandana in front of his face.

Four fans hanging from the ceiling did little to spread cool air from the inside air handler as humidity from the Chesapeake Bay wafted through the doors and gaps around electrical and lighting outlets.

Both lawyers kept their opening statements short, knowing there was going to be more to this trial in the forthcoming days; there was no sense in wasting their or the jurors' time.

After a few witnesses testified and were cross-examined, everything seemed finalized for closing statements and the jury to decide the case.

But Richie Granger had other ideas. He grabbed a device off a table and held it high in the air for the people to see.

The State's prosecutor, Jorge Melindez, rose slowly to object but then paused a few seconds to see what is was about.

And Granger started, "This is a tape recorder."

He walked around the front of the room proudly showing it off.

Possibly, if he had it the day before, he would not have been so proud, but when it showed up this morning from his girlfriend and private investigator, Marcia Lane, he had new life in a trial that seemed destined for failure.

Marcia Lane had come hurriedly through the courtroom doors and dropped it in his last lap ten minutes before arguments this morning.

Judge Burrow looked on with amusement -- wondering how a tape recorder could be relevant to this case, since it was not listed on the exhibits' list and the defendant's psychiatrist had labeled Bobby Hutchings as crazy.

Granger walked towards the jury box and flipped open the top of the recorder to reveal a tape.

Melindez had enough of the show and spoke up, "Your Honor. Counsel would ask what the tape recorder and tape has to do with the crime committed considering they are not on the list of exhibits."

Burrow looked at Granger and said. "Well?"

"The recorder device and the tape will show that Bobby Hutchings was coerced into killing Presley Whitfield."

With that, Granger walked back to his table and set the recorder down; he wondered if what he just said would get him thrown out of the courtroom or sanctioned.

Melindez then shifted on his legs to take some of the pressure of them: he had enough stress from 150 criminal cases on his desk and fifty bench warrants that were active for rapists, kidnappers, and murderers. He didn't need a monkey wrench thrown in the middle of prosecuting a confirmed killer in a murder case.

But he wondered if he was missing something -- in the detective's interrogation of the shooter, 24 year old Bobby Hutchings, who sat at the defendant's table with his head humbly bowed in his hands.

The man confessed, did he not? And his fingerprints were on the gun. Granger is going to look like a fool on this, so let him proceed.

"And why wasn't this item on the defendant's discovery list?" Judge Burrow asked.

"The recorder and tape became available in the last hour," Richie said, as he looked behind him in the courtroom to see if Marcia was still sitting in her seat at the back right side of the courtroom.

Sensing an outburst by the attorneys, Burrow asked them to approach the bench and said, "Both of you are to be in the conference room in five minutes and let's talk about this."

Raising his gavel and letting it fall slowly to the desk in front of him, Burrow declared the court to be in recess and asked the jurors to return in thirty minutes.

He excused himself from the bench and walked through a back door to his private stash of goods in a small closet – where he had soda water and crackers in a carryall pack.

He took the stash out, had a few bites of the crackers, and took a drink of the water; he shook his head a little and swallowed the mixture; then walked to a conference room and sat down in a chair.

The lawyers were waiting for him.

"So what's on the tape, Richie?" Burrow asked as he slowly chewed the away the last of the crackers.

"It's a silent sound recording. Well, let's say it's a recording of a silent sound."

"A silent sound?"

Burrow wasn't in the mood for playing games this morning – he had five contested cases on his docket over the next few days.

"Get on with it, quickly," he said.

"The tape that surfaced this morning has a recording that proves an external force emitted a low frequency radiation emission to Bobby Hutchings' head telling him to murder Presley Whitfield."

Jorge sat silently thinking about Granger's statement and wondered when Burrow would have enough of it and close the meeting. Surely, the judge would dismiss the tape and its introduction from the record.

But Burrow had seen enough of these cases to know there was some truth to Granger's introduction.

Jorge Melindez knew the technology was real--and he was getting sick of cases arriving on his desk. Mothers had killed their babies, rapists were stalking and killing women, and robbers said they heard voices telling them to break into stores and steal something.

"And you got someone who can verify this?" Judge Burrow asked Richie. "And where did this tape come from?"

"The tape was acquired from private investigator Marcia Lane, who went to Remote Tracking Services in Fredericksburg and got it from an electronics technician."

"So what relevance does it have to this trial?"

Judge Burrow was trying to stall some and not be partial to Granger's argument.

"Hutchings visited RTS prior to the shooting saying he was hearing voices in his head telling him to commit a murder. He had complained about this technology to his doctor, but nothing was done to investigate the source and get rid of the voices -- other than to prescribe some psychotropic pills which only made him feel sick and confused."

"Really?" Burrow said as he nervously began to shift his feet on the floor wishing the day were over.

"Yes, this is why I am amending the defendant's claim to being a victim of undue coercion."

Jorge stood up leaning against the desk with his hands on top. "You can't do that." Jorge looked at Judge Burrow. "I haven't received that pleading Your Honor, and I ask for that and the tape recorder be excluded from the record."

Richie was not about to stop talking, since he had come this far with an argument he was prepared for: he had the patent numbers of the technology devices, the maker of the machines being used, and the field studies that showed the applications of silent sound technology and the effect on humans.

And he had multiple parties supporting him.

Two non-profit agencies in support of physical and mental health had been calling weekly about the trial and asking what they could do to help.

But a silence in the room left Richie wondering what exactly he had gotten himself into -- when Burrow and Melindez were looking at each other speechless.

Richie thought back to when he had first accepted this case from Judge Burrow last month: the judge had asked him to represent Hutchings in a murder trial that no other attorney wanted.

Maybe if Hutchings had not screamed out to a newspaper reporter standing nearby that he was being unduly coerced with subliminal voices, when he was arrested, things would be different. Now the whole world knew about it.

Judge Burrow had said, "You're a good man who can take care of this situation."

Richie, sensing it was time to continue his argument, spoke up, "The technician's report says a recorder and a listening device aimed at Hutchings' head received low frequency pulsed modulated radiation emanations from an external force that told him to murder anyone that started to bully him when he left his apartment."

"And you have someone to verify this?"

"Yes."

Richie leaned back in the swivel chair, put his hands behind his head, and relaxed.

"The state hasn't allowed funds for expert testimony," Burrow said, nervously trying to feign support for Richie's position.

Riche knew this was coming.

"I'll pay for it," Richie said, knowing the two agencies were willing to help financially.

Jorge had sat down and started scratching his black short curly beard.

Finally, he spoke up, "Judge, this is ridiculous. The evidence has not been submitted for examination, his argument has no merit, and there's been no advance notice of his position. Again, I ask the recorder introduction be retracted from its record."

"Objection noted Mr. Melindez."

"Also, Judge, that is a federal issue and I would ask this case be moved to the federal court."

"You won't move it anywhere Mr. Melindez. The jurisdiction for this case is noted in your filing, and you know Circuit Courts have digression over some federal issues. I don't hear anyone here asking for a mistrial. Granger, send me something showing the validity of a recorder taping neurological emanations like what Hutchings may have received."

Richie nodded his head and smiled slightly. "There's one more thing, your honor."

Richie deftly picked up a piece of paper and held it up.

Richie waited for the questions but got none, so he spoke up, "My client's been micro-chipped."

Judge Burrow had enough of new revelations for one day and stood up while Melindez looked on in shock.

"Granger, amend your response as warranted. The state will have to defend itself from the allegations, if it decides to pursue the charge. For the time being, I'm declaring this trial a mistrial with all these new revelations. Now, if you will excuse me men, I will declare the mis-trial and release the jury and reset this trial for July. Get your complaints and additional discovery listings to me within thirty days."

And with that, Judge Burrow arose and went back to the closet for more crackers.

2.

During the break, Rufus Stronger and Marcia Lane had been sitting in the courtroom patiently. Rufus was reading a book while Marcia sat and looked through her calendar.

Both were tired from a week's activities of spying on people and travelling.

Rufus had been keeping his eyes peeled on Representative Tyler Harrisen, a Republican who had won a State Congressional seat in Henrico County.

An anonymous party had sent Rufus a $5,000 retainer check in the mail asking him to see what Tyler was doing outside of office time, so Rufus started tracking Tyler around the county. Rufus would also use a radio scanner to find the frequency of the Congressman's office cordless phone and check out some of the calls.

Considering Tyler had received financial donations from businesses that were profiting from his legislation in the State Assembly, Rufus did not have reservations about checking Tyler's incoming and outgoing calls. Besides, the $5,000 advance money that came in the mail in cash was nothing to sneeze at, and Rufus was in the investigator business.

Rufus would also be investigating Tyler's family relationships, real estate transactions, and memberships in clubs.

After all, politics is a social platform, and where there are rich and famous people gathering, there are politicians looking for notoriety, prestige, and money.

Meanwhile, Marcia, who had travelled to Fredericksburg to get the silent sound tape recording of Bobby Hutchings voice targeting from Remote Tracking

Services, had also been working three nights a week providing security for a storage facility.

But this court case was a big deal.

"The establishment would do anything to get rid of that tape," Richie had warned her before she left for the Fredericksburg trip.

"Well, it's worth a try," she had said. "I won't call first. I'll just go up there with a release from Bobby and get it. I'll charm my way in."

"That you can do."

3.

After the lawyers and Judge Burrow returned to the courtroom, the Judge forbade he jury to discuss the case with anyone; they were released from duty and told they'd be paid in a couple of weeks.

Richie sat at his table and gave Bobby Hutchings a pat on the back; then he hurriedly gathered his files and looked for Marcia.

Her eyes across the courtroom met his, and she got up and met him in the middle of the center aisle. They walked through the doorway and he led her to a quiet place in the lobby.

"I don't know how you got this tape but I sure hope it's the right one or I'm in deep trouble."

"It's credible. I played it on a recorder just to make sure. There were low frequency voices on there that talked about killing a man. Technician says another device makes the voices clearer and louder, but he certified the process took place on Bobby Hutchings two weeks ago, and he's willing to take the stand and testify. He was a former Signal's Intelligence analyst with the Department of Defense."

"Well, thank you, and if the judge determines it is evidence, I'll deal with that at the proper time."

"I'm sure you will. And now there's plenty of time to work on the case too, from what the judge said."

"There's still a lot of work to do. We'll need a copy of those papers Bobby keeps talking about, and the man's identity that was in his cab."

"Okay. Who do I bill this to?"

"My office. There are unlimited funds available from an Indian group who want this killing program stopped."

"You got it. Langley AFB here I come."

"Oh, I forgot about that."

"Well, that's who we're dealing with here -- when Bobby's cab let that man out at that booth."

"Well, see if you can find out something about the shady character and I'll go from there."

"Where do we go from right here?"

"To lunch. This court area is getting stuffy."

And Richie led her out the door. "Let's go out for a bite to eat."

"Is it legal to do that after a trial?"

"Honey, anything's legal when you know the right people."

Richie pushed out the perimeter door of the lobby and ushered Marcia onto the sidewalk.

"Glad I'm with you."

They walked to a cafeteria two blocks away on this hot summer day all the time wondering if someone was out to hurt them.

There had already been numerous instances of the same people being in their areas at different locations.

Two cars nearly hit them as they crossed an intersection, and a fire truck screamed by just as they were entering the cafeteria.

4.

After Judge Burrow declared a mistrial, Jorge
Melindez had went back to the conference room and sat
back down in the chair – he wanted to get his thoughts
together before walking back to his office at the justice
center five blocks away.

He was still in shock -- knowing if this surveillance
subject continued at a new trial--it would be stifled with
a state gag order or someone blowing up the courthouse
to prevent a super secret technology from making its
way to the public arena.

Now he knew why there was no request for a bail hearing from Richie, with the great tape surprise.

Five days had went by and there was no notice for a bail hearing; so he waited for some kind of preliminary hearing, but that was waived -- probably because of the surprise tape and a loaded countersuit which probably maintains the state was at fault for killing Presley Whitfield and using Bobby Hutchings as the murderer.

What else does Granger know? Melindez asked himself as he rose up from the chair and walked out of the courthouse. *Whitfield had connections to what? Jesus! What's going on here?*

While Jorge was walking back to the justice center, Judge Burrow had gone back to his cracker stash and took a seat for a minute in his private chamber to reflect on what had just happened. *Somewhere, sometime, I'll get these people back. If Representative Tyler Harrisen had not won this district, this case wouldn't even be happening, but here we are about to open up a big can of worms with short mouth Melindez as the state's prosecutor.*

Judge Burrow was not going to succumb to a politically appointed prosecutor like Melindez, and his young associate attorney -- who had been dressed in all black with a stack of files on a table that reached his neck at the plaintiff's table.

Judge Burrow had been passed over multiple times for judicial appointments to appellate, district, and federal court positions because of his independent ways.

He objected to political appointments and favoritism. He thought a best-qualified person should be getting a judicial appointment and be elegantly referred from a majority of ethical lawyers.

So what if his rulings were according to the law of the land and void of his personal opinion – his job was to enforce the Code of Virginia pursuant to the U.S. Constitution and not according to some lobbyist or politician trying to please a group of businessmen or rich entrepreneurs.

What happened to the days of appointing judges who had the best qualifications for the job? For Christ's sake, I'm 68 years old and don't have many years left. I don't give a damn who does not like my rulings or orders. What can they do to me? I'm probably the only judge who has had less than five decisions appealed to appellate courts in thirty years on the bench and never had any overturned. But here I sit in this circuit court listening to civil cases, that if two parties could learn to talk to each other civilly and work out a plan of compromise -- there would be peace. But not this one – this one will give the system a burp. Let's go for it.

5.

Bobby Hutchings, who had been sitting at the defendant's table, was returned to prison.

When he got there, it was recess time; so he went outer edge of the compound's perimeter and looked through a barbed wire fence to a river one hundred yards away thinking about life.

It wasn't unnatural for him to spend time looking at a river. He was born in a cabin that fronted a roaring river from the Carolina Mountains on the Reservation:

he had spent many days fishing, washing, and drinking from that river of life.

The white stones on the creek beds had reflected the sun's rays; the clear waters were smooth and soothing to his skin, and the wild greens that grew on the side of its banks fed his family in the coldest of winters.

That was life, only it was a poor life, and when there was an opportunity to escape poverty and travel around the world, he walked into a military recruiter's office and joined the Army.

Since he was good at making crafts and familiar with raw materials, he became a procurement and supply clerk, and the Army sent him to Fort Eustis.

He loved the waterways in this part of the country too, but certainly didn't expect to be caught up in a white man's struggle for power, prestige, and secret technology applications.

One day I'll be free. It wasn't me that committed that murder.

Just before trial, he had had a talk with his defense attorney Richie Granger, to discuss strategy for the murder charge that had been filed one month ago.

Bobby had told Granger all about the man blocking his path to exit the apartment enclave, where a couple days prior to the murder -- the man had threatened him if he didn't shut up or cough up the papers that had been left in the back seat of Bobby's cab.

The next time, Bobby would be would be prepared, and when the man came again and blocked the exit and came towards him, he pulled a gun out and shot him.

Granger had left satisfied with the story and said he'd be in contact with him in a couple days: there was going to be a trial by jury.

Sure the authorities had the gun and his fingerprints, but they had no evidence of how he was bullied into the killing the man. Somehow, he had to get the evidence heard and proved that he was being targeted.

When he saw Marcia deliver that tape recorder to Richie in the courtroom, Bobby's face had lit up like the county fairgrounds at night.

But now, he was in jail -- until the authorities let him go or he could prove that he lacked intent to kill and was no threat to humanity.

He probably shouldn't have agreed to the initial interview with the detective, but he was not a man to withhold truth; he trusted in God for life.

But slowly he was finding out God was not in the court system, and now he wondered if God was alive at all.

The detective had said, "Don't think God had anything to do with this Bobby."

"Well, someone did!" Bobby had vehemently responded.

Detective Brownlee looked at Bobby quizzically and decided to go along with Bobby's feelings. "Well, maybe the devil did it."

"Exactly," Bobby uttered positively.

"So until we get to the truth, we'll keep you and the devil in jail."

Bobby had said, "Right."

And he found himself in jail.

Bobby could have smacked himself after agreeing with the detective. *When will I ever learn?* He thought.

He turned around and walked back slowly towards the prison building all the time mindful of anyone out to hurt him. A conspirator could be in prison.

But most prisoners were at the basketball court, where a group of six men were playing and running the length of the court shooting the ball.

Before Bobby entered the door to the building, he kicked the dust off his shoes and brushed away any bugs or lint from his orange prison jumpsuit. The last thing he needed was for some kind of foreign material to be found on his bunk bed and be blamed for it. He did not need any extra cleaning work: he was already assigned to cleaning the dining area five days a week.

And he sure didn't want to be labeled as being crazy, which is what some doctor was trying to do when he had come to Bobby's cell and asked him a few questions about his mental state.

So Bobby was quiet about telling anyone he was hearing voices, until his cellmate, Shorty Beales, started on him.

Bobby entered his cell and Shorty was lying on the bottom bunk reading a book.

"Well, how'd it go?" Shorty asked.

"Postponed, as usual."

"But they had a sequestered jury, no?"

Beales was a small time petty criminal who got caught stealing jewelry from department stores and selling the stock to pawnshops, but with new tracking technology on jewelry, he had no idea the law was onto him, and he got caught and sentenced to two years in prison

"Yeah, but it was postponed. Judge told everyone to go home."

"Wow. That means you're in the clinker for another month and I got to live with you."

"You're a lucky man Shorty. Because when I get out, you get out."

"How's that killer?"

"Bobby started for Shorty's neck but paused when he saw a guard approaching to see if everyone had made it back to their rooms.

Kill him, the voices within said.

And then Bobby recognized the same command from the day of the murder, so he sat down in the only chair in the room to think about it.

"How's that?" Shorty asked again.

"Because when I prove I am being unduly influenced by some high tech gadgetry, I'm getting out."

"Well, comrade, there must be ten of us in here who have been unduly influenced and hearing voices telling us to commit crimes. What makes you so special to get released?"

"It's not me Shorty. That lawyer of mine's got some kind of deal to get this case heard. Says he believed every word I said. Said to 'hang in there baby -- might be here for awhile'."

"But I said, 'I want to go home'."

"He said, 'No, you don't, Prison is the safest place you can be right now'."

"I asked, 'Why's that?'."

"He said, 'Because they're on your side'."

6.

After lunch with Marcia, Richie Granger returned to his office and put the Hutchings file on his desk, and he sat back wondering what to do the next day.

The Hutchings issue was supposed to have filled the whole week.

He gave Marcia a call on her cell phone.

"Hi again. What are you doing tomorrow?"

"After some office work, I'll probably go to the country club and stalk Starr Hendricks."

"Rufus still got you doing that?"

"Yes, until the Hendricks' assets are divided and the divorce is finalized, but I like it. I have a membership and can go when I want to the club courtesy of Rufus."

"How nice, but how about a boat-ride on the water tomorrow? Will he let you off?"

"I think so, with a little charm. I'll tell him we're talking trial strategy on a cruise."

"And fish strategy. Be at Sam's boat ramp at 8:00. It'll be a good day to go since the winds are down."

"I'll be there. I'll pack some goodies."

"Great. See ya then."

Marcia loved being on the water. She started thinking about fishing, swimming, and feeling the salt air blowing across her hair to relax her nerves.

Richie left his office early and went home to get things ready for the boat outing. He dressed down to sweatpants and a tee shirt, and he drove over to a nearby storage yard to hook up his 18' Boston Whaler to his Toyota SUV and back it into his condo parking lot to check out the equipment in the boat.

Life jackets, toolbox, spare gas can, and an emergency kit were right where he had left them.

He went to an outside storage shed and grabbed four fishing poles, a tackle box, a net, and two crab traps. He laid the items inside the boat and then jumped up and got behind the steering column.

He turned the key to the ignition but there was no power, so he went back to the shed and got a battery charger and attached it to the battery.

That done, he went up to his condo and rested in the living room.

Life was good. The Hutchings trial was declared void for now; he had a wonderful girlfriend, a blossoming law practice, and money in the bank.

But that would change once word got out about him exposing the biggest secret since civilization began -- using electromagnetic forces to control people.

This time he would be ready, unlike in southern Hampton Roads when antagonists and released blackmailed criminals started harassing him.

The next morning, Marcia showed up at the ramp in a white short-sleeve cotton knit shirt and khaki shorts over a brown stringed bikini top and bottom. The bathing suit color went well with her blond hair, which by now in late summer, had been sun bleached from time at the pool.

She had parked her car in a smaller section separate from the boat and trailer parking area.

She saw Richie's Toyota and boat trailer near the launch ramp, where another man was unloading a small aluminum johnboat from a trailer.

Richie greeted Marcia and asked if she wanted to drive the Toyota or unhook the boat from the trailer.

She chose driving the Toyota, since she had never been in Richie's boat; so Richie put on the parking brake and let Marcia get behind the steering wheel.

Once the other fellow had unloaded his boat in the water, and his partner had pulled their vehicle and trailer up the ramp into the parking area, Marcia backed the Toyota and trailer down near the ramp that descended into the water.

Richie walked down the concrete ramp and released a winch lock on the trailer and a hook that went to the boat's front – all the time holding onto a rope off the boat's bow.

He sidestepped some protruding water and jumped onto the dock. He walked across the wood planks and stepped into the boat.

Since the boat and propeller was partially submerged into the water, he started the engine and let it run for a few seconds; the cool water would keep the engine cool.

Then he gave Marcia a sign with his hands to back the trailer down into the water a few more feet, which she had done many times with her dad's boat trailer at Bow Creek.

She let the truck and trailer naturally roll down the slope of the ramp and then quickly pressed on the brake to send the boat off the trailer and into the water and floating on its own.

"Hey. Easy on the lift off," Richie yelled out.

Marcia ignored the remark. It was up to him if he wanted the trailer backed further in the water and got the wheels wet.

Once she saw the boat floating backwards, she put the Toyota gear in forward and parked the vehicle and trailer in the boat section of the parking lot.

She was excited -- and had almost forgotten a bag of sandwiches and fruit stuffs she had in her car, so she walked to the car to retrieve the bag. She paid little attention to a truck with two occupants in it who had their radio blaring loudly and stared at her.

Richie had the boat swung around to the side of the dock, and a rope clove-hitched to a cleat.

Now she would confront him about the remark.

"Richie. If the boat trailer had gone back any further, salt water would have gotten in the trailer wheel bearings and they would have to be repacked."

"Oh. Hadn't thought of that."

"Case closed."

Marcia handed him the bag of goods and he sat them down on a cushioned seat as he grabbed her hand while she was stepping into the boat.

"Well, that went okay, huh?" Marcia said as she grabbed the bag and put the perishable items in the ice chest.

"Very good. I couldn't have done it without you, like a lot of things."

Richie backed the boat away from the dock and turned into the channel of the Chesapeake Bay.

It was a delightful morning with no wind, and the sun was rising over the eastern shore.

He motored the boat slowly through the no-wake zone while periodically glancing at a boat and trailer that was backing into the water at the ramp – mindful of any danger that may be lurking – after he had argued yesterday for Bobby Hutchings to be acquitted of murder and released from prison.

There were bound to be adversaries.

He had learned that back in Virginia Beach a few years ago when he was a representing a client who was simply trying to get worker's compensation for an injury suffered on the job – through no fault of his own.

The man's first lawyer had failed to file evidence from a doctor about the injury. Richie got the evidence and filed it in the discovery phrase of the case but became harassed at work, play, and home.

Whoever implanted Bobby would not want to be discovered – nor would a chipmaker that made the device.

He looked at Marcia and smiled -- happy he was on the water with her in the sunshine amidst geese flying overhead and loons diving for fish. Egrets were standing in nearby marshes ready to capture any stray minnows coming their way.

With a mild southwest wind starting up in the middle of the channel, Richie drove the boat to the mouth of an inlet a few miles from the boat ramp and turned the motor off on calm tidal waters.

He dropped anchor, and the boat stilled after drifting a few feet.

Except for the lapping of small waves against the side of the boat, it was quiet.

"Nice out here Richie," Marcia said as she opened her large carrying bag to get some oil and a towel."

"Sure better than being in the office."

"Or in town. There's so much pollution from all the passing vehicles, and God only knows what's coming out of the crematory at Shoreline's Funeral Home."

"Excuse me?"

"The funeral home. It's right in the middle of town, and there's a terrible smell coming from it on a northeast wind."

"I've heard that metal toxins can be released from a dead body," Richie said as he wiped water spray off a console. "Like mercury from teeth fillings."

"Well, maybe that's it, or dead flesh."

Marcia removed her shirt and shorts and got comfortable sitting on a cushioned seat area against the window of the boat. She drew her hair back and put a band around it at the back. She wiped some oil on her face and looked at the cooler.

"What kind of bait we got?"

"River shrimp and bloodworms, in the cooler."

Richie began to untangle fishing pole lines and started digging into a tackle box for bottom rigs and artificial lures.

"Shrimp's the best all around bait for catching something," he said.

"How about sharks? We might see some," Marcia said as she looked around to see if there was any other boat traffic in the area.

"That we might. I got something for them too."

"Lord, I hope so."

A few minutes passed while Marcia oiled herself and Richie's back -- while the frozen shrimp sat thawing in the sun.

"You're quiet today," Marcia said as she finished putting some oil around his facial area and chest.

"Well, yeah, with all that's happening in court, I guess it's a relief to be quiet. I'm sorry. Let's fish, enjoy the sunshine and the cool breeze before I get condemned."

"Nothing bad is going to happen to you Richie. God is always in control, and he wouldn't abandon something he started."

This is why Richie needed Marcia in his life; she was always the confident one, the one to say the right words at the right time, and could give him comfort when nothing else could.

"Right."

Riche baited a hook with a bloodworm and put a two-ounce sinker on a snap swivel and handed the pole to her.

He took another pole and quickly cast a non-baited dark surface plug thirty feet towards the channel. He set the pole in a holder and sat back while using another pole to troll for flounder.

After they caught a few small fish at the entry to the inlet, Richie looked up to see a boat had deviated from the main channel and was heading straight towards them, and it was not slowing down.

"Hold on Marcia! Might be a little wave here."

"Oh yeah. Nothing new. I'll get against the starboard side."

About ten yards from Richie's boat, the boat did a quick u-turn making a big wave that was sure to cause disruption and overturn drinks, the tackle box, and anything else that was not locked down.

In the back of his mind, Richie knew the boat would soon be in trouble with the 80-pound test line he had thrown on top of the water that would get tangled up in its propellers if any boat got too close.

As soon as the boat turned, it wasn't a minute before there was a whirring sound of its motor and the boat drifting to a stop in the middle of the channel fifty yards downstream.

"Victory," Richie muttered slightly.

"Very good Richie. How'd you manage that?"

Marcia nibbled on crackers and took off her sandals. She lay back on the forward section of the boat and watched the scene.

"Surface plug with a hook one foot under."

"Wow! And I thought you were just a great lawyer!"

"Not against the law to fish."

Marcia laughed and began to look in her bag for a mini-camera. After she took a picture of the boat, she went to Richie and gave him a kiss on the cheek.

"Well, good catch. I got sandwiches, potato salad, tomatoes, and watermelon. Just say when and I'll get them out."

"Hey, let's throw those crab traps out. This is a perfect place to catch them."

"Okay. I'll cut the heads off those two fish we caught and use them for bait."

"Excellent."

Marcia put a fish head in the middle of each wired trap and slowly lowered them by rope onto the bottom of the riverbed alongside the boat; then she tied off the rope and went back to eating her crackers.

"This is sure nice Richie, and I thank you for bringing me."

She spread her legs the length of the bow area and relaxed in the sun.

Richie just smiled, and he grinned even more when he looked out over the horizon and saw the troublemaker's motor boat had drifted further into the bay.

After a few minutes, Marcia saw the ropes from the crab nets moving on occasion, so she went to the side of the boat and pulled a net up.

It contained a couple jimmies – male crabs. And when she pulled up the other net, it had four crabs -- but two of them were under the 5" minimum shell length. She threw the small ones back into the water while the others went into the cooler. Any female crab that had eggs would also have to be thrown back into the water, according to the current law, which usually changed each year.

Richie had caught two flounder with his rig, and Marcia had several croaker and spot fish.

They decided to move further out into the bay but at the edge of the channel.

Richie immediately hooked into a red fish, while Marcia got a few more croaker. There was no sign of their enemies.

After lunch, they took a ride to Marlins Bridge and sat in the shade near a bridge support. The sun was high overhead and starting to heat boat and bodies.

They caught a few trout, and when the cooler was half-full of fish and crabs, they pulled anchor and headed nearer shore, where they dropped anchor and ate lunch without the boat rocking.

After lunch, they took some pictures of the marsh, egrets, and some dolphins. They fished a couple of more hours in this spot and were content to relax on the calm side of the shore now that the wind had picked up and the tide was moving.

Bodies tanned, cooler full, and enemies nowhere to be found, Richie thanked his lucky stars and turned the boat toward the ramp.

"There's quite of bit of fish and crabs in the cooler," he said.

"Great. Let's cook them."

"Sounds good, but I got to clean the fish first and wash the boat off with some fresh water."

"Okay, I'll steam the crabs while you clean the fish."

"It's a deal."

Marcia put her shorts and shirt back on and cleaned up the blood and fish residue off the boat's deck. She straightened items out in the cooler and secured a bag of trash.

Richie turned into the ramp area and tied the boat to the dock. Marcia jumped onto the platform and went to get the Toyota.

She got in the vehicle and backed the trailer partially down the ramp while Richie hooked the cable from the winch to the boat, tightened it, and got back in the boat and revved the engines to get the boat to the front of the trailer. He finished hand cranking the cable to bring the boat to the front of the trailer and locked the handle.

He motioned for Marcia to pull up slowly, while he elevated the propeller and went to the back of the boat to unplug a drain hole – for any excess water to escape.

Marcia pulled the trailer up slowly to a level area and stopped on the side of the road.

"Go ahead Marcia. Pull it over to your car area and we'll unload your stuff."

She drove the Toyota to the back of her vehicle and stopped, glad she was able to help out, but it was always satisfying to get back to shore and stable ground. It was worth it though, to have seafood to eat.

Her boss Rufus would certainly know, after spending years clamming in rough and shallow waters in rainy and hot weather on the James River.

The Allied Chemical spill however; which closed the river to shell fishing, had actually been a blessing for him – forcing him to change job occupations.

Richie dropped Marcia off at her car and thanked her for a wonderful day. And he gave her a kiss on the cheek.

"So, what time is dinner, chef?" Marcia asked as she let the window down.

"Oh, Lord. Give me a few hours, like at 6:00 p.m. Is that alright?"

"Sure. I'll go home and change into something different."

"Well, you don't have to, you know."

She smiled and said, "I do have to. I'll see you at 6:00."

She drove to her little apartment in Newport News – thanking God for a nice day and the protection he provided in the midst of bad people. Knowing him made all the difference. Prayer morning, noon, and night, confirmed her faith.

As Richie drove away from the parking area, he looked back for his antagonists but saw none.

He figured they were still unwinding the 80 lb. monofilament test line from the boat's propeller shaft somewhere downstream, but he did see their truck at the end of the lot.

That was good, because he could now get a license plate number and see who was out to hurt him.

He stopped, and drove slowly towards the truck, stopped again, and took a picture of its back end and license plate. For added identification, he drove up a few more feet and took a picture of the side of the truck.

7.

Marcia arrived home at 4:00 and took a quick shower to get rid of a fishy smell and residual sand and salt off her.

She lay down on the bed for a while and nursed her tired arms, which had tired from holding the fishing pole and bracing herself from some of the bigger waves.

Fishing was fun, but holding a pole, casting the line, and pulling fish out of the water could also be tiring, especially when it was hot.

She reached over the side of the bed and turned on a small fan, and felt the cool air hit her body. It wasn't often she could lie without clothes on in the late afternoon in the apartment, because people were usually walking around nearby, but on this weekday afternoon, not a soul was in sight. Fortunately, there were woods across from her living area. For a low-income apartment, it wasn't bad. She felt free and safe – for now.

She read a few chapters of a latest suspense novel by a licensee of Robert Parker, who had written eighty some books but passed away last year; some books were about a woman detective.

She got up at 5:00 and put on a cotton knit short-sleeve yellow shirt with a scoop neck, which had a pale blue bow in the middle. She wore bone colored shorts that were cuffed above her knees and flat neutral sandals with chestnut brown leather straps.

She looked at herself in the mirror and was satisfied: her weight was at 112 pounds and fit her 5'7' frame well; her long blond hair was smooth but still wavy and hung loosely proportioned on the sides of her head and behind her.

She walked over to a desk where she stored her creams and accents and put on an ivory tone lacquer finish on her nails. She brushed her hair. She also put on a swath of neutral semi-gloss oil of clay on her lips. With some of the excess, she added some pure olive oil and rubbed it between her hands lightly covering her face: the day's sun had robbed a lot of oil from her skin.

Life was changing by the day, and her faith was carrying her through. She loved her job, friends, and more than anything, her destiny.

She felt that had been established one day in deep prayer when she was alone at home and confused about life; but a vision was given to her of happiness and serenity, and she's never forgot it. If only she followed the dream, she would arrive at a destination of security and fulfillment.

Since she received that vision, she could see it coming true, as each obstacle in life would be overcome by faith and commitment.

Not everyone figures it out, she thought as she turned before a mirror to look at her sides.

It could have been much different--if she had believed the lies her mother was telling her – about never succeeding in anything or prospering financially.

But the people at a nearby church would encourage her, and it was there she learned about faith and work.

She was glad she had bowed to the truth years ago and moved on towards a future of becoming independent yet trusting in God for success.

But in this investigator's job, she didn't have quite as much contact with the poor and sick of the world, which really needed help.

She turned from the mirror and grabbed a rush woven multi-colored teardrop bag off a kitchen chair arm and went out the door.

She drove to Richie's condo in Williamsburg, all the time thinking about what the poor man must be going through for representing a confirmed killer named Bobby Hutchings' and confronting the state about covert targeting. *But certainly, he proved today that he could handle things.*

She arrived at 6:05 and walked up a flight of stairs to his unit and knocked on the door.

He greeted her, and he looked good.

His short black hair was combed to the side and his face was radiant from time on the water. The whites of his eyes were clear, and they surrounded the deep brown irises on both sides under lisps of dark eyebrows.

He had on a light blue-collared golf shirt and navy blue jogging pants. A hint of Old Spice lingered in the air surrounding him, as he bowed to hug her just inside the doorway.

She was wondering if he was going to let go, but she waited patiently, knowing he needed security and love as a man who had yet to find the full meaning of faith in life.

In the air, there was also a fresh aroma of seafood and natural salt.

The sun was bellowing its last light through the kitchen window, and a lighted candle was on the table that smelled of apple and pomegranate.

He raised his head and said, "You look nice."

"And you too."

She followed him into the living room and dropped her bag on an end table. She walked to the kitchen counter to check out the fare.

"Well, you've got everything done," she said as she put her hands on her hips and wondered what she could do. "It all looks so good. And you even got some sauce made up."

"Well, the convenience store had some made up. Anything to drink?"

"Actually, I think I'll settle for a glass of water. I do have some important work to do tomorrow, and Rufus was nice enough to give me today off."

"Sounds good. Help yourself, and I'll put the buffet on the table."

After they were settled at the kitchen table waiting for the food to cool, they talked about the weather and the wonderful day they had on the water – and of course the incident that could have drowned them.

"I got their license number on the way out," Richie said, as he started to eat some fried flounder.

"Well, that was a good idea. Rufus has some software at the office to find the owners of vehicles."

"Might put that on the calendar, along with getting Bobby Hutchings out of jail."

Marcia didn't know how to respond at first, but then said, "Only if he wants out of jail, but it may be the best place for him right now."

"Well, that's true."

"But if he is proven to be coerced by another party, he should be out of jail."

Richie stared at her intently – knowing what she said was right – but being right and proving it was another matter.

"I don't know if Jorge is going to pursue this matter or not, but I got a feeling someone will."

"When will you know?"

"Burrow has suggested thirty days to do something, and I suppose I'll hear from Jorge sooner than later."

A short pause ensued while Richie was cracking crab legs with a nutcracker and shedding the meat from the shells.

"But it really doesn't matter. I'll go on without him and file some kind of legal action against someone – maybe sue the state, if I can figure out who the state is," Richie said with slight frown.

"The devil has a way of raising his ugly head when the pressure gets too much."

"He does, doesn't he? But what does that really mean?"

"It means that there's a guilty man out there somewhere who will run out of places to hide and start talking – because he can't stand silence."

"So I just watch and see what happens?"

"Kind of like that, but just keep expounding truth and putting on the pressure. Look at one man recently in the news, who took off and tried to escape to another country but somewhere he'd read or found out that he could be a suspect in a murder trial and got found."

"Well, he must have made some mistakes."

"A life of crime makes mistakes," Marcia said.

Richie finished scraping some crabmeat from a main shell and discarded its leftover contents on another plate. He dipped the good meat into some horseradish sauce and savored it.

"Well, he might have figured out he was being pursued," he said.

"No doubt, but even if he didn't, God often steps in unknowingly and convicts a criminal mind. Look also at the Apostle Paul in the Bible: he was riding on a horse and got knocked off by Jesus in the spirit. No one was chasing him, except God."

"So both these men were wicked people who were going somewhere?"

"Yeah, on to more wickedness, until God stepped in and changed things."

"I think I understand. A man, a righteous man, just states what is righteous in front of the world and waits for a response."

"Exactly."

"Takes awhile though sometimes."

"Yeah, some people are stubborn to respond. But that's what makes it fun."

Richie knew he would never win this conversation and have the last word, so he quit talking and finished his meal, while Marcia ate the last of her croaker fillets and arose from the table and started clearing the dishes.

Finally, he said, "Thanks. That was a good allegory."

"Oh, you're welcome Richie. Don't worry. Everything will work out."

And she went over and gave him a kiss on the cheek along with a wet cloth to wipe his hands.

After they sat in the living room awhile and relaxed, Marcia said goodbye and went home.

It had been a long day.

If only every day was like this, she thought as she drove home. *Maybe one day, when I retire from work and have a loving husband.*

8.

Life had been somewhat boring after Marcia had acquired her investigator's license a year earlier with the intent of finding her stalkers and becoming free of cyber-stalking.

She was still watching Ms. Hendricks in an equitable distribution phase of a divorce case -- with Mr. Hendricks living in a run-down bungalow.

But when Bobby Hutchings' girlfriend, Starling Meeks had called her that morning -- after Bobby had murdered Presley Whitfield -- life and business would take on a whole different meaning.

Marcia remembered the phone call well. "Is this Stronger's Private Investigator Service?" Starling had asked.

"Yes, it is."

"May I see you this afternoon? My boyfriend has killed someone, and now he is in jail. I want to find the people who started harassing him."

"Sure. You're welcome to come to the office after lunch. How's that?"

"Great. I'll be there."

Unveiling of secret actions had few dimensions until Starling had called and Maria found herself embroiled in another cyber-stalking mission, but this was becoming a norm for her life.

After being cyber-stalked and chasing a stalker out of town and shutting down a major drug operation a year earlier, Marcia was well aware of the human targeting process and the players involved.

Bobby Hutchings' stalker was obviously another high-tech perpetrator.

From that phone call with Starling, Bobby's case would send the stalwarts of clandestine activities over a wall seeking refuge from a legal nightmare in a court trial that would just be the start. If the case was termed "precedential"; it would reverberate throughout the nation in due time.

Marcia was sitting at her desk in her office above Ward's Furniture, where she and her boss, Rufus Stronger, held counsel every couple of days about who to spy on next.

Rufus was her partner and had been in the investigator business for five years now. He had upgraded his transportation from a 1998 Buick to a 2017 Honda SUV. Quite a leap for a former clam dredger.

Marcia sat in her usual summer detective's uniform: a short sleeve blue cotton knit pullover shirt with navy blue shorts and t-strapped sandals.

But if she had to hit the street, or be disguised, she could reach into a bag of goods and come up with dark black pants and black tennis shoes. She harbored different colored hats, scarves, and gloves. White colors were a no-no, because they could be easily seen.

She was looking through the Hendricks file to see if there were any more assets she may have missed for the next court hearing, which would determine equitable distribution between the divorced couple.

It wasn't normally such work for a private investigator, but when two parties provided interrogatories that were full of lies and deceit, the lawyers agreed that an independent party should be assigned to account for the discrepancies; hence, Marcia Lane and Rufus were hired to find out who owned what and where.

Mr. Hendricks had won the divorce -- but certainly not the assets.

He was furious Mrs. Hendricks wanted retirement funds, alimony, and two houses.

But it was the boat that really got him -- a 24" yacht he loved to take out in the Bay with his friends to play a few games of cards and drink with crab nets dropped over the sides.

The wife said he could have the boat in trade for the retirement funds.

Over my dead body, he thought.

So there were many disagreements, and Marcia would have to track down titles, dates of purchase, and location of ownership.

Marcia closed the file and put it back in the lower cabinet. She sat back in her chair and admired the desk.

Shortly after Marcia had agreed to join Rufus in the business, he brought this solid wood desk up from the downstairs furniture store.

With a mahogany veneer top and three drawers on the side with a pull out board, the desk sat like an old relic just waiting to be shined. That she did, with lemon oil and wax.

There was also a middle drawer for immediate needs like pencils, paper clips, and staples.

Her .38 caliber pistol was in the top right drawer.

Every private investigator should have a gun, she thought. *Sneaking around people's homes and following them to hotels could get a person shot, in or out of the office.*

And then there was that knock on the door.

Marcia sat back looking at the door because it was partly open.

Seeing no one, she said, "Come in." *Maybe it's a disabled person and there is trouble getting in,* she thought.

A short skinny young woman dressed in a checkered flannel shirt and blue jeans, with long brown hair tied behind her back peeked through the doorway and softly asked, "Are you Mrs. Stronger?"

"No. I'm Marcia Lane. Mr. Stronger is my partner and we've yet to marry or change the name on the door downstairs. Come in."

"I'm Starling Meeks and I'm so glad to find you. I saw your card on one of the waiter's trays at Rosie's Café."

"You're a half-hour early."

"I know. But I just have to see you."

"That's fine. And what do you think I can do for you?" Marcia said, as she looked at a computer screen on her desk and wondered about the weather forecast for the weekend.

"Someone's trying to kill my boyfriend," Starling said.

Marcia didn't flinch. "Happens quite a bit nowadays with adulterous relationships, thievery, and slander gossip. Any of that going on?"

"Heavens no. Bobby and I have been together for years and he would never do any of that."

"Always good to ask first. I thought he was in jail."

It would be cloudy over the weekend with cooler temperatures on the way, the wording said on the screen.

"How do you know?"

"I'm a private investigator. I read the papers too."

"He is in jail, but that won't stop them."

"Could be right about that."

"He was a faithful man until this happened," Starling said with sadness covering her face. "Maybe we should just forget about it," sensing that Marcia may not be interested in her problem.

Marcia noticed her solemn face and asked, "Why is someone trying to kill your boyfriend? And I'm sorry if I have offended you. Have a seat there in front of the desk."

Starling swung her Vera Bradley cotton handbag off her shoulder to her front side and sat down gently on the black vinyl cushioned chair in front of Marcia's desk --while looking at a leather chair that was in the corner of the room.

Marcia noticed her glance and said, "That's for crazy people."

Starling smiled and began to relax.

"That is a nice looking chair."

"You like furniture?"

"My father used to upholster furniture, and I'd hold down the fabric while he stapled it."

"You might ask for a job downstairs in Wards. They can always use another worker."

"I might do that."

There was a silence that permeated the room for a few seconds while Marcia waited on Starling to get her thoughts together.

A clunk reverberated throughout the office from the street below when a delivery driver let a hydraulic loading platform fall to the pavement.

Marcia had heard the sound many times before and sat still, while Starling jumped.

"Just a truck on the street," Marcia said.

"Bobby had found something."

Marcia waited for more but nothing came, so Marcia spoke up, "Well, he knew where his gun was."

"Oh, you know about the murder too?"

"Yes."

"Well, he found a manila folder with papers in it."

"Oh, that was nice. Did he return it to the owner?"

"Well, it didn't say who the owner was."

"What was on the papers? What did they say? Were there numbers on the papers, drawings, facts, figures, names, or locations? And where did he find this at?"

"All that with headings like addresses, land coordinates, computer type language codes, foreign addresses, and a heading that said *Langley Air Force Base*."

"Wow. That narrows it down."

Marcia closed the computer program and turned the computer off.

She got up from the chair and walked over to the window to look at the street below for anything that could help her reality mood. It was a habit of hers, when something seemed out of the ordinary. Rufus did it all the time, and what Rufus did, Marcia did, because Rufus was smart and had been in this business a long time.

But then again, Rufus was hot for Sherry Linton, who was a waitress across the street at Rosie's Cafe. He'd kept his eye on the brunette haired lady ever since she started working at Rosie's and wearing one of those short red-checkered skirts.

Marcia turned towards Starling and walked across the room to get a cup of water out of a five-gallon jug on a stand. She didn't ask Starling if she wanted some, because Starling was not going to be there much longer. *Jesus, Is this some kind of a C.I.A. operation?* Marcia asked herself.

"And you think someone is trying to kill Bobby because he found this file?"

"Oh, I do, Mrs. Stronger."

"No, no. I'm Marcia Lane, not Stronger. Not yet anyway."

Marcia sat back down at her desk.

"After Bobby found this file, someone entered his apartment and rummaged through his belongings."

"He file a police report?"

"Yes. But that didn't stop the perpetrator from doing something terrible to Bobby."

"I thought he wasn't home when this break-in occurred."

"He wasn't home then, but two days later Bobby woke up with blood on his pillow feeling like he had been drugged somehow in the middle of the night."

"Interesting."

Marcia knew all about that because something similar had happened to her a year earlier. Rather than get into that, she sat back and let Starling talk.

"You see, Bobby operated a cab, and he picked up a guy at Parkland Avenue and took him to Langley Air Force Base. When Bobby got back to the station after his night shift had ended on a Friday night, he found this file of papers on the back seat and brought it home to look at it. He wondered if he could return it to the owner but saw the information and got scared. He hid the file under the bed mattress, where the intruder did not look when he broke in. Then the next day, he took the file to the bank and put it into a safe deposit box. Anyway, after the intrusion, a couple of days later, a man tried to bully Bobby at the bottom of the stairwell of the apartment building where Bobby lives, and that's when Bobby pulled a gun and killed him."

"And what would you like me to do about all this?"

"Find out who owns that file."

"Might find that out from the victim's associates."

"Bobby's in the Peninsula Detention Center in Hampton. May I have some water, please?"

Marcia got up and gave her a cup of water.

69

"Our rates are high here, Miss Meeks," Marcia said as she walked to the water jug. "You have money to afford them?"

"Lots of it," Starling said, as she took the cup of water.

Marcia smiled and said, "Well, okay. I'll need a $1,000 retainer fee, which will be pro-rated and returned to you for any work not done. A check with your telephone number and address on it will be fine."

Starling opened her handbag, got a checkbook out, and promptly wrote a check.

Marcia got Starling and Bobby's personal information and started a file folder.

"Can you get me a copy of those papers the man left?"

Starling had said, "The papers should be in that safe deposit box at the bank but I don't have access to it."

"Get access. Ask Bobby to give you a statement that gives you permission to access the box. He'll have to have his signature notarized, so you may have to take a notary with you. But I need a copy of those papers. Better yet, while you're there, make three or four copies."

"Okay. I got one more question," Starling said as she rose from the chair. "You know a good lawyer?"

"I do, but he mainly practices product liability."

"Well, my boyfriend's a product, and right now he's a liability."

"I'll talk to him but can't promise anything."

"Thanks."

And Starling got up and walked towards the door.

"Bye Starling. You try and have a nice day and be safe. Watch the heavy door on the way out and the thugs on the street. You got any protection on you?"

"A can of mace," she had said.

"Good for dogs. May need to upgrade a little," Marcia said, as she put the file folder in the drawer and made notes about the case on a scratch pad.

Then Marcia picked up the phone and called Rufus Stronger.

9.

Marcia told Rufus the story about Starling and Bobby
Hutchings.

"Sounds like a good job to me," Rufus had said.
"Does she have any money? You get a retainer?"

"I got a $1,000 dollar check. Said she's got plenty of
money."

"Wow. Better check it out at the bank before you get
too excited, and definitely get a copy of those papers. It
would be nice to have a location of where the cab picked
up that passenger who had left the papers. Go by the cab

company and see what you can find out," Rufus had said.

"Okay boss. I just wanted to make sure you wanted the job."

"Well, it's your baby. I'm busy following this politician around and checking out his acquaintances."

"Bound to be a lot of them, See you later."

And Marcia hung up the phone.

And then she called Richie.

His secretary, Margaret, answered."He's in a meeting right now with something important going on."

"Is there another woman?"

"Good Lord, no. Someone murdered someone," Margaret said, as she looked at her desk calendar for any appointments to cancel or postpone.

"Happens a lot nowadays. Lady just came here at the office complaining about her boyfriend being in jail for murdering someone."

"Same one probably."

"But Richie does product liability cases."

"Like I said, something important is going on. Anytime the judge comes by here on his lunch hour with a stern look on his face, something is up."

"I've been out of the loop since I quit my job as a transcriber and don't know the attorneys very well. Who else would you recommend for representing this lady's boyfriend?"

"Well, there's Malcom Bridgers, who practices criminal defense law at the Bay Commons Center -- or Branton Quintley at Commerce Square."

"Okay. Would you ask Richie to call me if he gets a chance?"

"Certainly. It won't be long."

"Okay. Thanks, and I'll talk to you later."

Maybe Richie is already involved in this case somehow, she thought.

She got up from her desk and walked over to the window to think about things.

A cabby picks up a man, drops him off at Langley; there are papers in the back with names of people and personal information, and some kind of codes and radio frequencies, and plane arrival and departure times. Is this an espionage ring of some sort?

Below on the street, there were people walking on the sidewalks, a pet dog was sniffing residue in the gutter as the owner pulled his leash, and rock doves walked along the curbs looking for food.

She didn't see Starling anywhere.

Her thinking was interrupted when the phone started beeping, and she went over to the desk to pick up the receiver.

Noticing the number, she said, "Hi Richie. How are you today?"

"Fine, fine. Just a little busy. Margaret said you called."

"I did. A lady came by the office and said her boyfriend had killed someone and needed an attorney. I told her I'd try and help her find someone."

"Wouldn't be a Bobby Hutchings, would it?"

"Well, yes. How did you know?"

"Between you and me, I was asked to take on the case, though there are several fine attorneys around here that represent murderers."

"That's because you're good Richie. You should consider it an honor."

"Or a curse. I don't know a lot about criminal defense."

"The state wants you bad enough, they'll provide you help."

"They will, won't they?"

"Be a good opportunity."

"You available?"

"Only on weekends."

"That would do."

10.

So Richie had been assigned as counsel for Bobby
Hutchings and met with him in the prison's visiting
room at 10:00 Thursday morning three weeks before trial
in the Circuit Court.

Richie wanted distinct information on events that
had happened before Bobby shot Presley Whitfield in
the hallway of an apartment building.

Bobby was in his orange jumpsuit and sitting down
on a metal chair at a five-foot long wooden table when
he walked into the room.

Richie sat at the opposite side, looking good in a black suit with blue tie and white shirt.

Richie laid down an enclosed file folder on the table and asked Bobby how he was doing.

"I'm okay. Even made a few friends here, and a few enemies."

Richie said, "Well, that's normal so far."

Richie relaxed and took out a small voice activated tape recorder from an attaché case and laid it on the table.

"Okay. Tell me in detail the events that led up to the murder."

"Look, I'm just a cabbie, okay? I work ten hours a day for four days a week on a late night shift and go to Fred's for a beer on Friday night and Josie's for breakfast three times a week. I got a call on a Thursday night to pick up a guy at Parkland and Juniper Streets -- a shady looking character with a bowler hat and dark suit. I drive 14 miles to Langley Air Force Base and let him off at the little booth there in front of the base. He gives me the fare and a $5 tip. When I get back to the station and clean out the car, there's a file folder on the back seat that I presume was left by Mr. Shady. Being the uneducated man I am, I took it home and looked at it the next day; inside were papers with people's names on it, addresses, insurance policy numbers, and ages. There were code numbers beside each name. There were eight pages of these names. There were also plane rendezvous times, passenger lists of about twenty people and some destinations listed – a few pages of them. I'm not sure what the last pages were with biological, genetic, and cultural code numbers along with primal tribal affiliations and descent origins. But it was all kind of spooky and interesting, so I put it under a book and forgot about it. A week later, my apartment was broken into but nothing was missing, that I could tell. But late one night during that week, I got sick from something I ate. And then I began to put two and two together -- that someone may be after that file and want to get rid of me. So I put the file in a safe deposit box at the bank until I could figure out what to do with it – maybe make a little money with it. And then in another week, I awoke to find myself inflamed all over with a terrible headache and blood on my pillow and what felt like injection marks behind both ears. I started hearing voices, music, and crackling in my head."

Richie sat back and relaxed and took a few deep breathes. He reached over and turned the tape recorder off. He looked at the clock on the wall and saw there were twenty minutes left of visitation time. A guard in a dark blue uniform walked by as he looked through the wired glass safety window.

He sat up and said, "Here what is happening. The trial has been scheduled to start in three weeks, so we've got to get going on getting some evidence. My assistant is going to get the records of your passenger pick-ups and let-offs. Maybe she can even find the guy. But we'll get the times you were at different locations, plus some video that supports you being stalked by these guys.

Richie turned the recorder back on.

How did that passenger pay?"

"Cash."

"Who knows what may come out of the woodwork. The man you killed had a criminal record – and more than likely was being used to scare you into giving up those papers. Guess that didn't work, but obviously he was there to pressure you into giving up that file or make you forget about it. Now we need to find out who is behind it, who entered your apartment, and who is targeting you."

Richie turned the recorder back on.

Bobby spoke up, "Another week passed and I was going to my doctor for help. I left my apartment on May 29 around 4:00 p.m. and walked downstairs to exit the building when a guy was blocking the door. I had seen him a week prior when I was picking up a regular daily customer outside of Roger's Grill at the patio there. That man knew I was going to be at that location at that time, because that's a daily stop of mine. I kind of ignored him at first, but he still started at me. So anyway, when he was in my apartment building blocking the exit, I asked him to move, and he didn't."

"Was there anyone else at all around at this time?"

"No. The other tenant who lives at the top of the stairs works until 5:00, and the two tenants downstairs are hardly there ever."

"Okay. Go ahead."

"He stared at me for a few seconds and then another man came through the exit door and stood in front of it. They looked at each other for a second, and the first guy nodded his head at the other and they began to approach me. I backed up and pulled my gun, but it did not stop the one man from approaching. The other man took off when he saw the gun. I took my time, because I had been so angry at people stalking me all over town that month and at my job, I had planned to get back at whoever started this -- and I shot the man that was approaching me perfectly in the chest."

"You got a permit for that gun?"

"Certainly."

"Then what did you do?"

"I looked at him for a few seconds. The guy was still breathing, but at least he wasn't approaching me, so I left him and went to the store, which is about a ten minute walk from home."

"And when you got back?"

"Oh, man. There were police everywhere, and naturally, I was a suspect because I lived there. When they asked me if I knew anything about this shooting, I told them I did it. They handcuffed me and took me to jail. It was going to happen, and I had told the authorities it was going to happen, but no one would believe me and get me help. Someone has done something to me, and I've been hearing voices ever since

I woke up one morning with pain in my head and blood on my pillow. The targeting got extremely worse after I went to Dr. Doebe one day, and I reported these events to Representative Harrisen. Now I think I've been used to get rid of that man and me."

"May be. You got someone to take care of your apartment?"

"Sure. My girlfriend Starling goes over there and checks it out some. She stays there sometimes."

"Suggest she might put a new lock on the door with the owner's permission."

"Okay."

"Can you keep me in my current cell? I don't want to be mixed in with the general population – those bullies may have friends in here."

"No doubt. I'll ask about it. That's it for today. I'll be in touch next week," Richie had said, and he gathered his belongings, nodded at the guard, and exited the prison facility.

Bobby went back to his cell where his cellmate, Shorty, was waiting for him.

"Get any free cigarettes or anything?" Shorty had asked.

"That was my lawyer, not the cigar man I met."
Bobby had said.

"Both blow smoke," Shorty said, and he laid his head
back down to sleep.

11.

After Bobby had dropped him off that night at
Langley AFB, Willard Osmond walked from the cab to
his quarters satisfied he was making money off victims
of non-consensual experimentation, cyber stalking, and
sex slave services.

More and more people were being covertly drugged,
and the suppliers of the drugs were funneling him
money for every new name he put on a list.

It wasn't a coincidence Rep. Tyler Harrisen had
offered him the opportunity to sell young adults for sex

services– after Tyler had coveted monies from Willard in a buildup to be elected Representative for the County.

No. Tyler owed Willard some favors, from providing college girls looking for money in exchange for physical satisfaction, during years at college.

One thing led to another, and Willard found himself in the prostitution business, which progressed into kidnapping and experimenting on victims with some new technology – after the victims were drugged.

Tyler, in return, had influenced monetary grants from the Health and Human Services Department of the Federal Government to be given to doctors who prescribed synthetic neuro-toxins for their patients, and a Dr. Doebe was a participant.

In a few more months, Osmond would be rich, with kickbacks from doctors, a lawyer, and drug suppliers.

Rendition flights transporting young adults to foreign countries to become sex slaves however was becoming taxing on his nerves and wallet. Unneeded expenses for plane storage fees and paying off Air Force security personnel, for allowing him to use the military airstrip for rendition flights in the middle of the night as a ghost contractor delivering critical medical supplies, could land him in prison for life.

He should probably reduce the cargo load totals on the flight manifests to avoid suspicions.

He had arrived at his temporary quarter billets at 10:30 p.m. after the cab had dropped him off at the gate. He had entered a single room area and set his satchel on a chair -- and lay on the one cot in the room.

Normally, this was a rest area for pilots and crew who were stopping over for a night's refueling or having maintenance work done on a plane.

He lay and thought about the recent names that were added to the list, and he wondered if any of the girls would like him – the list provided by Presley Whitfield after Whitfield had stalked poor and humble young adults for drugging and kidnapping.

Whitfield was an errand man for Representative Harrisen and clearinghouse contact for a group of twenty lawyers in the Peninsula area that forwarded names of single women, abandoned children, and disabled seniors who were flush with cash.

He reached for his satchel to grab the list -- only to find the file was not in the satchel.

He sat up on the bed quickly and looked around the room – first at the one table and chair – and then all around the cot area -- but the list was nowhere to be found.

He got up and walked back and forth thinking; then he thought about the cab and the papers he had taken out of the satchel to inspect them. He had obviously left them on the cab seat.

This is not good, he thought. *Nothing can replace those papers! They were typewritten on a manual typewriter!*

He could not deliver the codes that had been assigned to each person for the upcoming holiday weekend to an information specialist that would upload them into a computer--that would monitor and control the victims' thoughts, moods, and actions by satellite targeting.

Willard was responsible, and it would be a mistake he would surely regret.

He had grabbed his phone off the table and called Whitfield immediately -- but only got a messaging service.

He left a message, "Presley, something is wrong. I left the list in Cab number 21 of Fred's Cab Company tonight! Find the driver and those papers! And contact your man!" he said.

Willard lay down and tried to nap, but sleep did not come because rapid thoughts crossed his mind about the list.

He got up after an hour and dressed in an airman's flight suit, gathered his satchel, and walked out of the billet section to the Gulfstream waiting for him.

The plane was loaded with 15 people according to his co-pilot, Jean Leichner, a German citizen and former pilot with the Blitzkrieg Command in Germany.

They would arrive at Frankfurt in eight hours, if the weather was good.

In the morning, Presley Whitfield had heard the message on his phone and thought to himself, *I am not about to contact Representative Harrisen.*

He'd take care of this issue himself. He'd find the cabbie's address and get the papers back.

Whitfield got the name of Bobby Hutchings from a clerk at Roger's Grill and found Hutchings' apartment.

He jimmied the door lock and went into the apartment on a night when Bobby was working, but he could not find the papers.

Got to make him sick or crazy or something, Whitfield thought.

So the next week, Presley broke in again and drugged Bobby's drinks and foods in the refrigerator.

Yet Bobby looked fine when he picked up a customer one morning at the grill.

The next week, Presley had decided to get tough and confront Bobby at the bottom of the stairwell, when he knew Bobby would go out for a walk – only to have a gun pulled on him – and the trigger pulled sending him into an unorthodox light of confusion and terror.

12.

When Richie had got back to the office Thursday afternoon after that first day of trial at the courthouse, Margaret looked at him quizzically and said. "That was a quick trial."

Richie smiled and said. "Gets that way when new evidence shows up."

Richie briefed Margaret on the conference room chat with Judge Burrow and Melindez.

"Speaking of Jorge Melindez, he called and wants to talk about something."

"I'll bet he does."

Richie walked into his office and picked up the phone. He punched in the numbers for the state prosecutor's office on the telephone keypad.

Melindez, expecting Granger's call, answered.

"Jorge, this is Richie Granger."

"Oh, hi, hi. Yeah, we're letting your boy go temporarily."

"Don't think so," Richie said nonchalantly.

"What do you mean 'don't think so'. Doesn't he want out?"

"No. Out is not the issue," Richie said, as he began to eat some beans and macaroni of what food what was left on a takeout plate from the cafeteria he and Marcia had visited.

"Oh, come on. You know you don't stand a chance of getting your petition through."

"Didn't know we were holding court on the phone Jorge. Is the Judge here or something?"

There was silence for several seconds before Melindez thought about how to answer -- maybe to give in a little on the case, seeing as it could be a self-defense issue with Whitfield having a gun in his pocket and a criminal record.

"A manslaughter charge would reduce the severe penalty of him spending life in prison."

"I'll remember that Jorge. Now if you'll excuse me, I'll finish my lunch."

"Yeah, okay. Talk later."

Richie hung the phone up thinking, *May be making some progress here.*

Richie mused over his options to free Bobby Hutchings from jail and get the charge of murder dismissed.

It would not be easy, considering law enforcement had the murder weapon with Bobby's fingerprints on it and a confession. After the autopsy of Whitfield, authorities would also have the bullet matched to the gun and shell.

But this was no ordinary case, considering Bobby had sought help for his mental condition and now had x-rays to prove that something was interrupting his thought process. Something was trying to control his actions and thoughts by some kind of remote neural monitor program and electromagnetic wave propagation – with intent to modify his behavior and kill someone, according to Bobby.

Upon research, these symptoms were indications of a C.I.A. Government funded program with grants secured under the guise of finding ways to defeat a foreign power in time of war.

Programs Monarch, MK-Ultra, Artichoke, Bluebird, and a host of others had preceded this current technology – having been used on Native Americans and unwitting victims. That, he had learned, from when Marcia was targeted.

But possibly, it was more than that.

During research, Richie had found there were victims in the United States who said their targeting extended to their family trees – from the beginning of American colonization to the present day.

Many victims had complained on certified videos that their mothers, fathers, grandmothers, grandfathers, sisters, and brothers exhibited signs of being mentally disturbed and had been treated for such conditions at some time in their lives – when at one time or another – there was nothing wrong with them.

If Marcia had not experienced such trauma months ago, Richie would not have believed what he was reading. But after seeing her suffering from being stalked and terrorized with some force of electromagnetic energy that a technician had measured to be extreme, he believed.

But what were his options?

Of course, the Fourth Amendment guaranteed a person to be secure in his own person.

But coercion in the form of electro-magnetic energy and microwave propagation would be hard to prove, not to mention radio signals being used on an otherwise healthy and normal person.

The term "undue coercion" was usually used in estate proceedings, where an invalid or elderly person had been coerced by another party to sign over assets.

Yet coercion could be produced by a threat of physical harm – to get a subject to do something -- that would not otherwise be done.

If receiving signals to the head by an outside party is not coercion, then what is? Such communications can be tuned in and remotely sent to sound like one's own voice or music – the Army's research papers said of mind control programs.

I will definitely need an expert to testify about this unless I can identify the chipmaker and the computer program associated with targeting someone. And getting the patents will certainly help.

And who is Presley Whitfield? The Shady character in the cab Bobby had dropped off at Langley? And just what information is on the papers that Bobby found?

Richie was asking himself these questions while sitting at his desk on a hot Thursday in Williamsburg, Virginia, in July of 2022.

After eating, Richie walked over to a file cabinet and retrieved his latest product liability case where a sidewall fell off a brand new tire and the occupants in the car suffered fatal injuries when the car swerved into a ditch and rolled over.

The tires had been made in Indonesia. If part of the sidewall had not been found on the side of the road, the defect may have never been discovered. But a passenger had heard a loud pop and asked a paramedic to search the area.

The paramedic had gone to the rear of the car about fifty feet, where there lay the rubber tread outer section of the tire and its sidewall: rubber glued bands which had been torn away and now stuck up out of the dirt with exposed steel wires twisted around the inner tread lining.

The paramedic noted this finding in a logbook.

Richie checked the manufacturer's on-line webpage and found that tread spacing thickness and width for tires were adjusted for different climate conditions: the tires would have to be mounted respective to climate conditions in different parts of the country.

Richie was wondering what study recommended that. *How could such a tire be truly balanced?*

13.

At Richie's request, Marcia began searching the county's register of deeds web page on the Internet for people who owned homes in the Parkland Avenue and Juniper Street area of Hampton, Va.

Interestingly, Tyler Harrisen's name came up as the owner of two multi-unit apartment buildings.

Marcia lifted her eyebrows and made a copy of the location of the buildings and the addresses. Then she searched for who lived in the buildings.

Presley Whitfield lived in Building No. 1 on the bottom floor in Apartment #2.

Holy Moly, thought Marcia. *Here's the connection.*

She navigated the cursor back to the search box and typed in the apartment numbers and the address of 5218 Juniper Street.

Three names came up, but it would take a small fee to get any information. She would have to ask Rufus for permission to use company funds for the information.

She decided a personal visit to the apartment area would be better, but first she wanted to have a talk with the manager of the cab company.

She called Starling Meeks at the flower shop, where Starling worked as a florist.

Viola's Flower Shop was only four blocks from Marcia's office and used by the community quite frequently for ordering flowers for holidays, funerals, weddings, church services, and parties.

Starling, just back from walking across the street to donate old flower vases to the Salvation Army's Thrift Shop, answered the phone with a greeting that said, "Where daisies bring praises and daffodils big thrills. Viola's Flower Shop."

"Well, that's a wonderful greeting, Starling. My boyfriend could use daffodils."

Starling giggled and said, "That greeting always gets comments Mrs. Stronger?"

"Marcia Lane, Starling."

"Oh yes. I keep getting the wording mixed up from the office door panel. What can I do for you? You need flowers?"

"No. No. This is business. I need to know the name of that cab company Bobby worked for."

"Fred's Cab Company on 17th St., next to the Newspaper building."

"Okay. I'll go over there and see what I can find out about Bobby's passengers."

"Great. Would it help if I call them?"

"Well, yes."

"I'll do it as soon as I get a bow on this new order. Lot of people getting married this time of year, you know?"

"I'll bet. Oh, and don't forget about the papers."

"I'm going to see Bobby at lunch tomorrow and try to get a note that gives me permission to get into the safe deposit box. You think there will be trouble?"

"There's always trouble. Stick to your guns and have your pepper spray ready."

"Downwind."

"Excuse me?"

"Downwind. I'll walk on the north side of the road to the bank."

"Ohhhh. So the wind doesn't blow the spray back in your face from a frontal attack and the prevailing wind."

"You got it. Wind is always coming off the Bay on that side of the street. I'll call you when I get the copies. May take a couple of days though."

"Yea, sure, Starling. Thank you so much."

Girl's not dumb, Marcia thought, after she hung up the phone.

Marcia got up from her desk, holstered a gun, grabbed a file folder of notes, locked the office door, and went downstairs to the parking lot and got in her car.

She drove to Fred's Cab Company, right next to the newspaper building, where Starling said it would be.

Fred Fulton had started the cab company shortly after he got out of the Army when he couldn't find a job.

One thing Fred could do was drive vehicles: cargo vans, jeeps, tractor-trailer rigs, and even tanks.

Red had been in a transportation unit at Fort Eustis, just down the road. So when his military enlistment term expired, he had a couple of cars at home that he modified into cabs, outfitted them with money mileage meters and braces along the doors with a separator panel between the back and front seats. He rented a small garage that used to be a vehicle body shop, and suddenly, after passing out some calling cards, he was in business.

He was sitting at a desk just inside the garage door when Marcia walked up to him.

She introduced herself to Fred and told him why she was there.

"Oh, yes. Starling just called and said you'd be by. Fine man, that Bobby, and now he's in jail. Could always depend on him to get here and leave on time with his cab cleaned up. How long you think he's in for?"

"A long time as it stands now. There are some extracurricular things going on with Bobby. His life could be in danger if he got out."

"Oh? Like what? He was pretty straight from what I know."

102

"Yes, Fred. But being straight doesn't mean trouble won't come around. It may even invite some."

"You got that right lady," Fred said as he looked down at a computer screen that showed each of his three cabs in different locations of the city. It was the first of the month and most calls were either going to or coming from the two Army posts in the area.

Marcia asked Fred is she could see the records of Bobby's pickups.

Without saying a word, Fred opened a desk drawer and removed a file folder.

He opened it and found a sheet of Bobby's pickup times.

But there was no copy machine available. Red always had to go over to the newspaper building to get copies.

He said, "Stay right here. I'm going over to get a copy of this and Bobby's logbook entries."

Marcia looked around the building while he was gone, wondering if anyone would be able to get in and search the cabs.

But it was secure, with only one dirty window high above the floor and a metal slide door fronting the road.

Fred returned and handed Marcia copies of the records.

"Thank you, Fred. I'm going to try and get to the bottom of this and get your man back on the road.

"Sure would appreciate it. People have been asking about him. Regular customers, you know?"

Marcia waved goodbye and drove to an empty parking area about one mile away in front of a closed church. She always felt safer near a church, and besides, God Almighty might reveal something to her that she may have missed.

Marcia shut the engine off on the car and looked at Bobby's journal to see he had picked up the shadow man at 9:10 p.m. at Parkland and Juniper streets. He dropped the man off at the entrance to Langley AFB at 10:15.

After a little break and prayer, Marcia took off to the intersection of Parkland and Juniper Streets.

She pulled up to a stop sign, saw there was on-street parking at the apartments, and pulled into one of the parking spots in front of 5218 Juniper. There were two sets of two story four-unit apartment buildings on the east side of the intersection, and a housing development on the opposite side.

Nothing looked unusual – there weren't any shady looking beer joints or dark windowed buildings – just two story apartment buildings and houses.

She got out of the car and took a panorama set of pictures of the area and buildings from the intersection. She also took pictures of address numbers on the buildings and street signs.

She went into the apartment enclave at 5218 and saw four mailboxes for the tenants – with the names of the occupants in small letters. The name "Whitfield" was on one label. The other names were Jones, Torreys, and Osmond. She wrote each of them down on a piece of paper and went to the next apartment building, where she wrote down the names.

Then she got in her car and went towards Langley AFB -- the way Bobby most likely would have gone – straight down Freeman Boulevard to I-64.

She looked for any businesses along the road that might have surveillance cameras pointed towards the street. There were a couple of convenience stores on the way, and she memorized the names of each of them.

When she exited I-64 and drove to the entrance of the Air Force Base, she slowed down trying to figure out the story she could tell an attendant to get on base. *I'll just tell him I'm an investigator trying to find the passenger in a cab, on the night of May 14.*

When she arrived at the booth's entrance, there was no one present.

Well, this certainly makes it easier. Bet if I got out of the car and started banging on the door, there'd be somebody here. Which means there must be a surveillance camera here somewhere.

She paused long enough to see a single round lens camera located at top of a front eave.

Now if she could only find the technician in charge to see the images of the cab and the passenger of May 14.

She drove to the first building that looked like an administrative office, parked the car, and walked along a sidewalk, mindful that someone was probably watching her.

She entered the building through a set of double metal doors onto a shiny linoleum tiled floor that looked like it had never been walked on.

She checked the first office on the left, but there was no one there. She did the same with the next three offices, and no one was visible or seemed to be anywhere in the vicinity.

Maybe they're on a fire drill or something, she thought. She looked out the back exit door and saw no one.

Then she called out, "Is anyone here?" in the hallway, and no one answered. Yet the parking lot had quite a few vehicles in it.

She started to go up a set of stairs when a man down the hallway and asked her what she needed.

"I'm looking for someone who came here a month ago. Is there a locator service here or Public Affairs Office?"

"Well, there is a public affairs office across the street, but the other buildings are for Air Force personnel."

Marcia was wondering if the shady man was a military man or civilian.

She thanked the man and walked over to the public affairs office.

Bobby had described the man as 5'10"tall with medium brown hair, an unshaven face, and dressed in a black sport coat, jade green silk shirt, and gray pants.

That doesn't sound like a military man. Maybe he was going on a trip? She thought. *"An aircraft. That's what information was on the papers.*

She got back into the car and went past the Public Affairs Office looking for the flight control center near the runway. She wanted to see the flight manifest for the week of May 12-19, if they would let her.

The flight center was in front of the airstrip – a north-south concrete pad that stretched from Interstate 64 to a field on its southern end. The building was yellow and weathered with iron oxide marks streaking down the sides from under guttering. Windows surrounded the upper half of the building.

A jeep appeared behind her with the lettering M.P.s, on the front of its hood, but she didn't worry about it. She wasn't doing anything wrong – just visiting the Air Force Base if they asked her.

She stopped in front of the yellow building and walked through the front doors, where she saw a man at a desk.

She greeted him and said she was a private investigator looking for a man who may have come here late on the evening of May 14.

The man was hesitant at first, but rather than make a scene, he looked at her investigator's license card and figured he'd release the information. His conscience was already bothering him about late night flights with groups of people boarding private aircraft and taking off to foreign countries.

He looked through a logbook for the month of May and saw two private flights had left in the morning of May 15, one with 17 passengers and 2 crewmen, and the other with 15 passengers and 3 crewmen.

"Can you give me the names of the people aboard and the destination?" Marcia asked.

"No, I can't."

"I could subpoena them," Marcia added to get the process moving along.

"It wouldn't help."

The man quietly looked at her and said, "I don't have that information, but I will make copies of these flight manifests and you do what you want."

"Great, Thank you."

He made the copies and gave them to Marcia. She thanked him and took off back to Newport News smiling and thankful she wasn't locked up in jail at Langley AFB.

Rufus would not have liked that.

She would ask Rufus to get the surveillance footage from the booth. She could be in trouble enough, as the M.P. vehicle followed her to the front gate.

14.

The next day, Starling woke up to see her mother walking around the house in a nightgown looking under chairs and tables – for Sylvester the cat.

Starling went into the bathroom, relieved herself, and looked at herself in the mirror. Her face looked tired, with darkness under her eyes and drooping cheeks.

Bobby had been in jail for two weeks, and it was taking a toll on him and her. He was not eating the food at the jail because he said it was too mushy -- and Starling, missed his companionship and jokes.

She washed her face and hands and went back to the bedroom, put on a pair of olive green scrub pants, a pale yellow open neck blouse, and two small wooden rings on her fingers. She grabbed a pair of tennis shoes and wandered to the living room. Sylvester was looking in the room from the outside window, but Starling said nothing. Her mind was on meeting Bobby today at the detention center during visiting time after lunch. She had to get that statement saying she could have access to the safe deposit box.

But would someone harass her on the way? She asked herself.

The last couple of days had been difficult, with some man looking through the flower shop window and staring at her. Another man followed her when she walked to Rosie's Café for lunch.

And why was mother was aimlessly walking the floor while Sylvester was eerily watching from the window?

Christ. Maybe they drugged something in here too, Starling thought, remembering the trouble Bobby had.

Those papers must be hot stuff!

Her mom finally saw her, and Starling murmured a hello greeting.

Any more than that would send a volley of words streaming from an overflowing mind of guilt, fear, and paranoia. Starling was freaked out as it was.

Starling wandered into the kitchen and grabbed an empty bowl off the kitchen counter and sat down at the table and poured some Cheerios.

She needed cheer. She reached from the chair over into the refrigerator and retrieved a small milk carton she had picked up yesterday.

Money wasn't the issue here in this household: it was jealousy. Anything Starling looked at, touched, felt, or spoke of – is what her mom turned into an avalanche of cascading sentences designed to throw guilt around the corners of the room.

What jealousy and interest could consume such a person! Starling thought as she spooned the cheerios into her mouth.

Starling finished her cereal, put the bowl in the sink, and walked back to the living area to grab her purse. She said a quick bye to her mom and walked out the door smiling at Sylvester who calmly looked at her and yawned.

It was a bright sunny morning with the sun shooting through tall oak trees and reflecting off home fronts.

It was three blocks to the flower shop.

When lunchtime came, Starling called one of Bobby's buddies to take her to the detention center, where Bobby had a statement prepared for her.

She retrieved it through the small glass opening of the wired bulletproof window, talked a little while with him and threw him a big kiss with some encouraging words; then she got back in the cab and went to the flower shop to finish her shift.

When she got back to work, she thought, *well, that was easy. Now I just have to get the papers from the bank. Tomorrow, if the cat is still outside and mom is consumed looking for it.*

15.

The next morning Starling lifted her tired body from the bed and found the bathroom. Standing up most of the day at the flower shop was taking a toll on her legs. Maybe today, she could sit some and decorate some baskets, before walking the few blocks to the bank and getting copies of those papers.

Her mother was snoring like a tired soldier, lying on the couch with her head tucked in the corner and her arms crossed on her chest.

Thank You Jesus, Starling thought. Not that she didn't love her mother, but the time consumed pacifying her interests and problems could take hours, to no avail. Maybe a slight resolution would surface as to getting mail on time, or keeping the neighbor's dog out of the yard, or her cousin Ethel from calling late at night wanting to discuss the latest political scandal. It was too much, and precisely why mom was laid out on the couch at 8:00 in the morning.

Starling dressed and walked to the flower shop slowly – mindful that someone could be out to hurt her.

She did want to see the creepy shadow man caught and Bobby out of prison.

However, she was not going to take a chance walking to the bank: she would use Bobby's cab friend, Jensen, to take her.

At lunch, he came, and he dropped her off at the bank. She walked inside and gave the account manager the note – and told him the story about Bobby.

He verified Bobby's signature on the affidavit and walked Starling into the vault area, where she went to Bobby's box and opened it.

The papers were still there. She turned and asked the manager if he would make three copies: one for Marcia, one for herself, and one for Bobby.

He did, and she left the bank and got back into Jensen's cab – relieved that nothing bad had happened.

She took one of the five page copies and folded it up. She put it in an envelope that she had addressed the previous night to Marcia Lane's Post Office Box at Shore Station in Newport News.

When Jenner dropped her off at the flower shop, she walked fifty yards to a mailbox at the corner of the street and dropped the envelope in it.

There, she thought. *Now it's the Post Office's responsibility.*

16

Marcia Lane was sitting at her desk this morning thinking about how Dr. Doebe was connected with putting a tracking device in Bobby Hutchings head.

She had learned from Starling that the doctor was Bobby's Ear, Nose, and Throat doctor at Waters Medical Building in Hampton.

But that didn't explain what gave the doctor motivation to implant Bobby.

She got up and went to Richie's law office to get a subpoena for Bobby Hutchings x-rays of a scan the medical center had taken soon after Bobby had complained about hearing voices.

But Marcia would love to interrogate Dr. Doebe herself -- and learn about his knowledge of microchips and effects upon the human nervous system.

Margaret had the subpoena ready for her.

Marcia went to the medical center's administrator's office and showed it to the clerk at the desk – without saying a word.

The clerk immediately opened her computer and found information about Bobby Hutchings and Dr. Doebe.

Bobby Hutchings had visited the doctor on three occasions. Bobby, in all three visits, had complained about ear, nose, and throat problems – with severe congestion alongside his neck and right ear canal.

Doebe had sent him home twice – with only prescriptions for medicine to relieve the inflammation.

The third time, some minor surgery was performed to drain the ear and reduce pressure, according to the doctor's report.

But there was another report from a clinical technician and X-Ray administrator a few days later. It said Bobby complained he was still having problems and wanted some x-rays taken, which was performed.

Dr. Doebe had no knowledge of Bobby getting x-rays at an office in the west wing of the building.

The clerk made copies of Bobby's medical records and made a phone call requesting copies of Bobby's X-rays.

In a few minutes, the X-Rays arrived in a protective envelope and Marcia cradled them in her arm with the other file.

Marcia thanked the clerk and walked out of the building, hoping she had the right copies.

17.

Dr. Doebe was battling his emotions after hearing that a private investigator had been in the next building requesting Bobby Hutchings records by subpoena.

He knew that Hutchings had killed a person.

And he also knew that he should not have implanted Bobby Hutchings with a cochlear implant and microscopic antenna.

But when a middle-aged man walked into his office prior to Bobby's last visit and threatened him with license suspension from the medical board and office closure, Dr. Doebe gave in and performed the procedure.

It was only a small receiver put near the ear canal with a biologically inert antenna to pick up remote transmissions from the electrical grid and cell phone towers.

But Doebe didn't know it was designed for Bobby to kill someone.

Doebe knew the day was coming when schizophrenic labeled people would realize that artificial substances had been injected into them to make them sick, go crazy, and hear voices.

The whole medical industry is nothing but a scam, with the military using electro-magnetic wave propagations to make people sick and label them as paranoid schizophrenics in combination with toxic food additives and chemicals sprayed that contain aluminum and barium particulates. So why did I join this profession? He asked himself this question as he sat at his desk in his office.

Because of my dad. Programmed to be like the great Herbert Doebe, Head of Internal Medicine at Hampton General Hospital and graduate of Eastern Virginia Medical School.

Dr. Doebe rose from his chair and looked at his certificates of achievement on the wall in front of him. Ten long years had passed from when he attended school to learn about a profession that could be summed up in one word: manipulated. *My God, the Indians knew better, using the herbs in the field grown by God to heal sickness. If only they had spiritual salvation from the great plant father, but maybe they did in their own way,* he thought paradoxically.

He walked past an associate nurse's office to a water fountain and took a long slow drink, trying to refresh his mind and thought. There was no one nearby in a waiting area.

He continued to think about his situation of being on call at all hours of the night, sometimes having to go to remote areas to service patients, and having to deal with subordinate personnel issues, which was occupying more time than healing people since there were applicants for administrative positions who had false credentials, drug problems, or criminal records.

At least he was out of the Emergency Room at Hampton General Hospital, where night after night kids were showing up with gunshot wounds to their arms, legs, and stomachs: it was making an ungodly mess everywhere.

General practice had its issues too: congested lungs, inflamed organs, and cancerous tissues resulting from excess drug usage, alcohol abuse, and food pollutants.

Concentrating on ear, nose, and throat issues were fine at first, but then he realized inflammation was the main cause of most upper body problems, and drugs and contaminated foods were usually the culprits.

But hearing voices is nothing but artificial targeting taking place to the skull, ears, and vocal chords.

Two ENT's had recently died for some strange reason.

Maybe it is time to quit, or at least change professions. But I won't have to quit if I testify about someone being micro-chipped: either the mob will kill me or I'll get fired.

But I sure will miss the pretty women here, he thought, as his nurse walked by in a tight uniform.

18.

Marcia examined the flight manifest she had gotten at Langley while Rufus was opening mail and posting debits and credits in an accounting journal. To heck with posting financial records on a computer: Rufus liked to see the accountability of his business on handwritten paper and cash receipts.

"The flight manifest has arrived," Marcia said proudly as she held up the paper above her desk trying to get some attention.

"And just how did you get a listing of flights at Langley AFB?"

"Charmed the guy at the counter of flight control," she said proudly.

"Didn't have to promise a date or anything?"

"No. He gave it to me willingly."

"Wonder if Sherry across the street would be so kind?"

"Depends on what you're asking for."

With that, Rufus got up and walked over to the window to see if Sherry was working.

"He just gave it to me," Marcia said with a sly smile.

Rufus wasn't impressed. He turned his head around and said. "You've probably been given something fake."

"You think?"

"You know how we get used sometimes."

"Maybe. Oh, yeah. Like last time, when we were guarding a warehouse that was being used for a drug operation."

"Right. So go slow on what you think might be a scoop or critical information. The investigator's license is not a free pass to just go anywhere anyhow and get anything. We're not getting paid for that."

"Plus, we got a reputation," Marcia said.

"Right."

"Well, I thought the shadow man might be a pilot or something, since he has not been described as a military man with a short haircut or shiny black boots."

"He may be, but the video surveillance will tell us that from the booth. Give me some time and I'll get it."

"Rufus. Is this our first argument?"

"We're not arguing. We are getting our priorities straight. And no, you got the chocolate doughnuts at the stakeout of that warehouse months ago."

"But you ate more."

"Well, I'm the boss, and that's the way it goes sometimes. Stay focused on the job. There's no judgment fund or bail money to get you out of jail at Langley or anywhere else."

"Right. Besides, we know Captain Tellis at the police department."

"Tellis would leave us in the clinker for sure."

"Not me. He likes me," Marcia said.

"Well, I'm not as pretty as you. We don't want to get into anything too heavy here. I mean jeez, M.P.'s following you around Langley is something we don't need."

"Maybe they thought I was pretty."

"Probably. Good way to meet the police chief," Rufus said.

"You mean *Commander*," Marcia said.

"You know, you're right. He would know about the surveillance system at the booth. If I can't figure out who's watching the booth, I'll call him."

"Well, there could be a Director of Security."

"That too," Rufus said.

"This manifest says two private flights left Langley on May 15."

"And?"

"Says a Dassault Falcon 7x took off with 17 passengers and cargo under 1000 pounds."

"What else?"

"A Gulfstream G650 left at 3:00 a.m. with 15 people and 500 pounds."

"Drug load must have dried out or got reduced. Must be going to Europe with the power of those tin cans."

"Got some kind of code in the destination block."

"The pilots names on there?"

"Just initials: A 'W.O.' and a 'V.M.'.

"File it and let it go, before we both get locked up. Here's something more interesting," Rufus said as he had gone back to sorting through mail on his desk.

"You got Sherry Linton's picture there?" Marcia said as she giggled slightly.

"Leave Sherry out of this. I think she's got a boyfriend anyway."

"Another lover never stopped most girls Rufus. Women always expect another man knocking on the door. That's just nature."

"Reminds me of an old proverb. Every woman has three men: one in her words, one in her heart, and another in her arms!"

"There you go," Marcia said.

"Like to be in Sherry's arms," Rufus mumbled as he sat back in his chair relaxing.

"Now, now. Stay focused on the job."

"Exactly."

And Rufus looked back at the mail and brought the chair towards the desk and studied a letter closer. "This one's addressed to you, with a return address from Starling Meeks."

"Ooh. Interesting." Marcia replied as she put the flight manifest in a file folder.

Rufus took a tissue and put it over the envelope and handed it to her. "You never know, you know? Cut it open with scissors."

"Should I save the cut out portion?"

"No, No. We don't get that technical."

Marcia laid the thick envelope on her desk and got some scissors out of a drawer. She lifted one end of the envelope and cut it open, slipped out a set of stapled documents and put them on the desk.

"It's those papers Bobby had found. Starling has gone to the bank and got copies of them."

Marcia opened the papers to the front page. "All kinds of people's names and addresses on them."

"That will help. Probably ought to make several more copies. Send one to Richie."

"Wow. This is huge," Marcia said as she continued to look at the papers.

"Be huger if we find the guy who owned them."

"We'll find him Rufus. Be patient."

Marcia walked over to the copy machine and made three copies: she gave one copy to Rufus.

He looked the pages over briefly and said, "They look credible enough, or why would someone go all to the trouble to get birth dates of people, social security numbers, addresses, and all this other information on here? Guess we should at least check out some of the names to see if they are real."

"Okay. I'll do that."

"And if they are, there's a likelihood of something criminal going on here. Boy. Would Captain Tellis like to have this."

"Be an ace up ours."

"Be four of them up ours, and job offers of some sort. But hold onto one and high tail a copy over to Margaret for Richie to have -- if they check out. Could be ammunition to get Bobby Hutchings free."

"Right boss. Then can I go to the pool and watch the guys?"

"You watching Hendricks or the guys?"

"Both. Don't want to get in the way of any muscle man."

"Sure. But no more M.P.s following you."

"I'll leave my hair up and roll down my sleeves."

"Yeah, and cover your slender legs. You get the cabbie records?"

"Did, but nothing looked unusual at Parkland and Juniper streets. Bunch of apartments and a housing complex."

"Find out who owns them."

"I think I know. But first, I'll check these names out on this list. Could be someone is in danger."

She typed in a few of the names on the list in the computer.

The people were real, according to the white pages on the Internet.

But their addresses were scattered out a hundred miles from Hampton, Virginia.

Most of the names were female, in their late 20's. But there were kids as young as five, and old people as old as 70, from the seven names she had randomly typed.

Possibly this is a group being targeted, she thought, as she knew the same thing had happened to her last year.

She shut down the computer and grabbed a copy of the papers.

She would go to lunch and the country club after dropping the papers off at Richie's law office.

"And we need that videotape," Rufus yelled as she walked out the door.

Marcia yelled back, "That's your job you said. You don't want M.P.'s following me."

It was good to have someone to talk to, Rufus thought.

19.

Rufus sat back in his chair for a few minutes reflecting on just how far he had come in life -- from being a clam dredger to now having his own private investigator service with a partner.

Shortly after the James River had closed to shell fishing, because of the Allied Chemical contamination, Rufus had started working at the shipyard – only to be denied promotions because of the good old boy system.

He left that job and started working with a surveillance company.

They had him looking for shoplifters in department stores; then he guarded the perimeters of construction sites; and finally, he conducted surveillance of store employees suspected of stealing money. After a couple of years, he acquired a private investigator's license.

It didn't hurt him to know people. Rufus often spent time in coffee shops talking about legal cases, politics, and business. Those kind listeners would later give him work spying, delivering valuable goods, and unlocking keyless door locks.

Marcia was icing on the cake – providing a feminine perspective on jobs and being able to blend in a crowd when he couldn't.

Rufus was not a big man, but he could certainly take care of himself, after years of hauling up clams from the riverbed and dumping them in the boat.

He had to be agile to do that; his slim frame and narrow shoulders allowed him to turn freely in that boat.

His short and curly black hair was combed straight back from a high hairline on the front of his head.

He always had some puffy cheeks -- probably from all the doughnuts he ate.

Today, he had on a cotton crew neck navy pullover and black linen pants – warm enough to be comfortable in any situation yet cool enough for hot summer winds that came whistling through town.

He looked professional, and always kept his brown oxford shoes spit shined.

Of course, sleuthing in the midst of drug dealers, thieves, and murderers required different attire.

He had been known to dress down to raggedy pants, patched shirts, and an old ruffled hat advertising the N.Y. Mets baseball team.

He got up from his chair and walked over to the window, and he looked down at Rosie's Café. Sherry Linton was a pretty girl -- and might even make a good wife.

But then I couldn't fish off the wharf, play softball, or look at other girls, Rufus thought, as he stared through the window at Rosie's. *Heck with that. I've got a Director of Security to meet.*

He walked back to his desk and grabbed the Hutchings file. He headed for the door, but Marcia's perfume scent still lingered in the air, and he thought of Sherry Linton again. *Got to get out of here.*

He locked the door and walked down the steps to the parking lot. He got in his Toyota SUV and headed for Langley AFB.

When he got there, the booth was unmanned, but he also saw the surveillance camera at the top of the eave that Marcia had discovered: someone on the base had to have access to it.

He found the Public Affairs Office and introduced himself to a nicely dressed civilian man at a desk. He told the man about the Bobby Hutchings case, and the man directed him to the Director of Security at the rear of the building.

Rufus walked down the hallway and found the Security Director's office, but first, he stared at the plaque on the door.

The lettering on Rufus's door back at the office was vinyl, but here the lettering was genuine metal on walnut.

Quite elegant, he thought.

He knocked on the door and no one answered, so he opened it and slowly walked into the office.

Kermit Cochran, a good-looking airman, was sitting at a desk reading a magazine with his back to the door.

He turned around slowly, looking dazed, as if his mind was still stuck in the magazine in front of him.

Rufus introduced himself and showed Kermit a badge and asked if could get a view of the front entrance of the compound on the night of May 14 when Bobby Hutchings and a passenger arrived there in a cab.

Rufus told him the story about how Bobby Hutchings murdered a man and was now in prison.

He also mentioned an unknown man had left some papers in the cab that night, and the man had been dropped off here at Langley.

"So, is this a legal proceeding?" Kermit asked.

"Yes, it is, though trial has been delayed because new evidence has cropped up, like right here hopefully."

"Well, you have to sign a release form, swear by your bones and body the information will not be used for any commercial intent or alternative use other than for use in a legal proceeding only."

"I will, your honor."

Kermit walked over to another monitor and punched in a few numbers and waited -- while a dark scene in front of the booth area appeared with a date and time stamp at the bottom of the screen.

"What time you say that was?" Kermit asked Rufus.

"Approximately 9:40 to 10:30 p.m."

Kermit sped the video up until Bobby's cab appeared.

"It was 10:15," Kermit said.

"That proves that," Rufus said as he looked over Kermit's shoulder. "Have any other angle to see a man exiting the cab?"

"There's only one camera," Kermit said.

He reversed and forwarded the tape and slowed it down to get a look at the passenger exiting the back of the cab though the darkness limited identifying him. The outline of a man about 5'11" with a thin build and sport coat could be seen, along with a rounded cap on his head, and that was it.

"Can I have a copy of this episode?" Rufus asked.

"Sure, since you got a court case going on. I'd like to know who the person is also. Most people would have taken the cab inside the compound to an office building, air field, or some housing quarters."

Kermit saved a one-minute view of the video and made a copy; he gave it to Rufus on a flash drive.

"This is it?"

"That's it partner. Technology has come a long way. You got a program to open the file?"

"Yes, but this is for the lawyer, and that's who I'm working for."

"Just checking your intents pal," Kermit said as he reached for two clipboards on the wall. He handed both to Rufus and asked him to sign his name.

After Rufus signed the release form and a checkout register for the flash drive, Kermit said, "You can keep the flash drive. Government's got plenty of them."

"Well, thank you."

"Good enough mate. Have a great day."

"Thank you so much, and if you're ever around Rosie's Café, stop across the street at my office and I'll buy you some lunch."

Kermit nodded his head and went back to looking at his magazine.

Rufus took off to Richie Granger's office to deliver the video and good news.

20.

The day had turned cooler with a north wind stifling the warm humid winds from the Chesapeake Bay.

Vehicle traffic was light during the middle of the afternoon, with most of the workers at the shipyards and Army posts still working.

Rufus headed to Williamsburg and Richie's office. While driving, he thought about the old buildings in the old colonial town: the Governor's mansion, Raleigh's Tavern, and a smokehouse.

But it was the stocks that always got to him, knowing men's arms could be chained within the wooden braces and the men whipped for stealing horses, food, or tools. *Jail would better,* he thought.

Rufus arrived at Richie's office at 2:30 and walked in the door to see Margaret typing away on a computer with her glasses halfway down her forehead.

She always looked good, and it was no different today, as she sat there in a light blue buttoned up sheer top with a dark blue skirt that drifted below her knees accented by some beige roped heeled shoes visible at the bottom of the desk: sophisticated but plain. *Always a comfortable looking woman,* Rufus thought.

She looked up at him and said, "Well, hello Rufus. How have you been?"

"Fine. Fine. Just came over to deliver this media tape to Richie. It's about the Hutchings case, and the video on it shows a man getting out of a cab that Bobby Hutchings was driving."

"Okay, Rufus. I'll see that he gets it."

"My partner been in here lately?"

"She was. Gave me a pack of papers and some pictures."

"Good. Be sure to tell Richie what's in that file. Is there a new trial date yet?"

"Not yet. We'll let you know."

Margaret turned from the center of the desk and reached into a drawer to retrieve a check. She handed it to Rufus, "You have a nice evening Rufus, and thanks for all your work."

"Thank you," Rufus said, as he smiled and took the money. "I'll see you all later when we get more information."

He walked out the door, satisfied that he was doing what the lawyer wanted him to do.

Now, he would go back to checking on Representative Harrisen's transactions.

21.

After an early afternoon meeting with two of the victims in the car crash, Richie returned to his office to work on the Hutchings case.

Margaret had told him by telephone about Marcia and Rufus dropping off items that were pertinent to the case; he was anxious to see what they were.

When he arrived, Margaret greeted him and handed him an envelope containing both the papers and flash drive.

He thanked her and turned to go into his own office, but she motioned him to come back and look at the contents of another envelope -- a $10,000 check from CARES, Citizens against Remote Electronic Surveillance, a non-profit group that had called Richie immediately after he began representing Bobby Hutchings and sent a $1,000 donation.

Richie looked at the check. "People are serious about this," he said.

"Well, I hope so, because there's every indication people are being bothered by what they are talking about."

"Yes," said Richie while taking a deep breath. "And this helps! I'm thankful for it, because for one thing, if I need expert testimony, this will be needed."

"I'll enter it into the books and send a thank you note."

"Great."

"How'd the interview go with the tire crash victims?"

"Okay, but we need close-up pictures of that tire the medical technician wrote about in his report. The police may have inspected it."

"I'll get the reports from the police. Don't know about the close-ups. May be a job for Marcia."

"That's a good idea."

"I'll send her a message."

Richie walked back to his office and opened the envelope with the papers and storage device inside.

He inserted the storage device in his personal computer and opened the video file.

He saw Bobby's cab and a man exiting the back door, with a date stamp of 10:15 p.m. at the bottom of the video, which proved Bobby was telling the truth about the time he had arrived at Langley Air Force Base.

Then he looked at the papers, which had addresses of people throughout the state, along with several other bits of information and codes.

He thought maybe he should turn them over to the F.B.I., but that would invite more trouble into a case that already had enough of it.

Time would take care of some issues, and he knew Marcia and Rufus were probably working on relevant bits of information.

His case was coming together – proving that the man in Bobby's cab was trying to cover up something criminal, from which Bobby had found in the papers. Bobby was being targeted because of what he knew, and Doctor Doebe became involved when he implanted Bobby.

But who gave the orders to get Bobby implanted? He asked himself. *Who befriended, or threatened, Dr. Doebe?*

Richie walked back the front office and asked Margaret if she would conduct a light search of Dr. Doebe's history.

She said she would, and he went back into his office to examine the recorded testimony of the female victim in car #1 at the car crash, who had heard a loud pop, just before the car had swerved and rolled over into a ravine pinning her against the steering wheel and smashing her leg into her chest breaking the bone.

22.

Marcia woke up to a stormy morning and looked forward to going to work. She wanted to hear what Rufus had to say about attending a fundraiser for Rep. Tyler Harrisen the previous night.

She went to the bathroom and brushed the sides of her hair over her ears. She put a hairpin on each side. With what hair was left over, she combed it up and let it lay back over the sides and brought it all together with a band around it.

She glossed her lips and rubbed her face with olive oil. She picked up a bottle of spring scented menthol powder and rubbed the powder on her arms, chest, and legs. Something about the medicated powder kept her cool throughout the day, and if there were any mosquitoes flying around, it seemed to keep them in check.

It was a steamy humid August morning with intermittent rain falling as she looked outside the window wondering what to wear.

She was happy she did not have to report to a stuffy courtroom to dictate a judge's order or transcribe testimony like she had done for three years.

She put on a lightweight black short sleeve cotton knit top and a pair of black nylon pants with cargo pockets. She put her cell phone in one pocket and a small .38 caliber pistol in the other.

She walked into the living room area and slipped on a pair of dark brown leather tennis shoes – ones that were waterproofed and would keep her feet dry.

She felt well. At 5′ 7″ and 117 pounds with narrow shoulders and a slim tanned face with light brown hair, she had confidence that she could attend parties with dignitaries, sneak into a bar to hear the latest conversations between adulterated lovers, dig a ditch, or run a ½ marathon. She had her body, and more important, she knew God. *What more could a person want?* She asked herself.

She sat at the kitchen table and said her prayers this morning for safety, wisdom, and performing work to the best of her ability.

The working woman is worthy of her hire.

She had a bowl of oatmeal, brushed her teeth, and grabbed a black shoulder bag off the couch that had been filled with snacks, notes, and personal finance and health needs. She always packed fish oil supplements and some tea bags.

She went out the door and got into her car. She drove to the office downtown. As misty as it was, traffic moved along well, and there were no accidents or back-ups on the way.

She always looked forward to seeing Rufus. They had some differences, but he was full of self-effaced humor and very smart about life and people.

Marcia was still learning, especially about how devious people could be.

Oh, she had a little experience in her childhood home, when her mother made silly excuses for going out at night rather than staying home with all three children. Marcia just thought her mother had something important to do – but later found out her mother was sleeping with other men.

"Don't wait up for me Marcia," she'd say. "I got some business to do with Sam, or John, or Damon."

And her Dad: when he got home from a six-month deployment on the open seas in the Navy, he made every lame excuse possible to go out with the boys three nights a week and drink alcohol and party at bars.

Deceit is what she had grown up with, until she had found that Episcopalian Church down the road and people of truth.

Oh how that wisdom saved me many times, she thought.

The first thing she would do when she got to the office was to get on the computer and perform an Internet search for a connection between Presley Whitfield and the shadow man: there had to be something linking them together.

Rufus was already at the office when she arrived.

"Morning pretty," he said.

"It is. Good morning Rufus, How are you?"

"Doing okay, after a seafood buffet last night."

"And how did that go?"

"Very interesting, in the bathroom."

Marcia quietly sat at her desk waiting for him to say more about that.

"Okay Rufus. You want to tell me, or this is private confession?"

"Thought that would get you. The shadow man has arrived."

"Praise the Lord. Hard to keep a secret."

"They tried, but old Rufus here managed to put down a well dressed scallop and scurry to the corner to see the action."

"And?"

"He looks like the figure in the Langley video, and he met with Tyler Harrisen on the way to the john."

"How interesting. You see a payoff or something?"

"No, but something was going on. And I got a sneak picture of him as he was leaving. I want to compare the video. May be nothing."

"They're all connected Rufus: Shadow man, Whitfield, and the Rep are all connected it appears."

"Hey. That's something. Let's check some yearbooks at the schools."

"Well, from my research, Harrisen owns apartments at Juniper and Parkland, Presley Whitfield's address is there, and now we just have to find the shadow man's real name and address. Still got to check the rest of Harrisen's tenants."

"Great. And that's about all we can do for now. Can't go around chasing chipmakers, proprietary composites, and needles."

"Might at least figure out what the stuff is made of," Marcia said.

"Yeah, and what the bottom of a grave looks like. Like Clint Eastwood said, 'A man has got to know his limitations'."

"I think that's when he was holding a gun to a man's head in a Dirty Harry movie."

"Exactly. After you get through, get that data over to Richie's office as soon as possible. And there was a message from Margaret asking you to get a close-up of a tire in the ditch for the accident victims Richie is representing."

"I know where it's at. I'll get it on the way."

"Great. I'm going to look for some lapel cameras at a store. The mini-camera last night almost got stuck in my coat pocket."

"How about a belt camera?" Marcia asked.

"Be fine if I didn't eat so much."

"Well, good luck boss."

Marcia began her research of tenants at the addresses of Tyler Harrisen's apartments.

Typing in apartment numbers and street address, the name of Willard Osmond came up at Juniper Street.

And she thought about the initials "W.O." – on the flight manifest sheet.

23.

When Willard Osmond had arrived back in the states a month later after having let off captive and drugged teenagers for sex slave indoctrinations in Germany, he bought a newspaper from an outside stand near his apartment to see that Presley Whitfield had been murdered and a mistrial had occurred in the Bobby Hutchings' case.

What in the world? He thought. *How could this be when he was plainly murdered? I thought Whitfield was going to take care of him.*

He returned to the apartment and sat thinking about things.

His bags were still packed in the apartment, and his clothes from last night lay on the couch. Cigarette smoke hung in the air like a bad fog when hot air meets cold.

Only he was the one that was getting hot – and worried.

As he sat on a couch, he reached over and stubbed another half-smoked cigarette in an Italian gold-rimmed ashtray on the coffee table. He reached for the paper again to verify the article. It said the same thing: "Mistrial Declared in Hutchings Case".

Osmond had made good money in human trafficking and drug dealing, especially in Germany where hashish was plentiful and men coveted American women. He had plenty of contacts at Langley that could get him back to Germany.

He needed to think fast, and he had to contact Tyler Harrisen about what was happening.

Tonight, Tyler Harrisen was having a fundraiser at a local restaurant, and Osmond wanted to pressure him.

Osmond wasn't a donor -- he was Tyler's controller – for the purpose of pleasing a worldwide organization of former intelligence agency criminals who thrived on power and secrecy.

Tonight, he would be Tyler's enforcer. Something had to be done to shut down this investigation of Presley Whitfield and Bobby Hutchings.

If only Willard had some contacts at the prison where Bobby was being held, he could make a deal to get Bobby beaten or made sick, but he had none.

Willard could harass Bobby's girlfriend, but what good would that do, when the damage was already done.

No. He would get Tyler to use his power over the prison to see that Bobby Hutchings never got out or got so deathly sick he couldn't think straight.

But what about the girl? She must have the papers. Or maybe Bobby's attorney has the papers.

He made a plan to see Tyler privately.

He got dressed in a dark brown silk shirt, black pants, and a black car coat.

It was 6:00.

He made sure his apartment door was locked securely and got into his car and went to The Lighthouse Restaurant – where the dinner was being held.

He got out of his car at the far side of the parking lot and walked slowly past the vehicles that occupied six long rows in front of the restaurant.

He told the hostess that he forgot to make a reservation but loved the Representative and to please find him an empty seat.

She took him to a seat in the back of the room.

He looked around to make sure nobody had recognized him in his new toupee and unshaven face.

Tyler was sitting at a table with seven other people when he saw Willard, and Willard motioned for him to get up and take a walk.

Tyler got up and headed to the bathroom.

And Willard followed him.

"What are you going to do?" he asked Tyler.

"I know. I know. We'll figure out something. The prison is a place no one should be let out."

"Might work, but how about the girl and the doctor?"

"You know Doebe. He's alright, I think."

"Thinking ain't good enough. Will he squeal about the implant?"

"I don't know," Tyler said as he smiled and moved out of the way of a passing man.

"This is a mess," Willard said.

"Give it time. Should pass over."

"Not with a new trial, it won't."

"Better close up shop then."

Willard looked at Tyler with indignation. "Listen, I put you here. This is your problem and I expect you to squash it. Do you understand?"

"I didn't lose the papers."

"Things happen. Just do something!"

"Yeah, yeah, sure," Tyler said, as he left Osmond and went into the bathroom while Willard left the restaurant through a side door.

When Tyler got to his office the next day, he called the prison warden and said there was a problem funding this year's salaries.

The warden was surprised – but not shaken.

Then Tyler started talking about Bobby Hutchings, and asked about how he was being treated.

The warden knew what the representative wanted -- and agreed that Bobby should be harassed in some way.

Tyler said that the funding might be all right after all.

But the warden could not have cared less about Representative Harrisen. The warden was going to retire in six months and walk away from being blackmailed or threatened by a politician.

When Willard arrived back at his apartment, he sat down and wrote a letter terminating his lease. He began to re-pack his suitcase and take pictures off the wall. Tomorrow, he would have the electricity turned off.

It was time to go, because he would eventually be found out as a co-conspirator in the murder of Bobby Hutchings.

Besides, he liked the tall brunette Whitfield had drugged and put into a van and then the cargo hatch of the aircraft that went to Germany.

The next morning, after a trip to the bank and with suitcase in hand, Willard Osmond called a different cab company other than Fred's and went to Langley AFB to find a free ride back to Germany.

24.

Marcia sat at her office desk looking at the flight manifests from Langley again along with the names on the lists from Bobby's cab. On her desktop, she laid printouts of Rep. Harrisen's apartments and her handwritten notes of who lived there.

And then it struck her again that W.O. could easily be the Osmond name she had seen on the mailbox in one of the apartment buildings.

Marcia continued her search on the Internet for Whitfield, Osmond, and Tyler Harrisen – and found a yearbook of juniors at Madison High School in Newport News with all of their names in it: Presley Whitfield, Tyler Harrisen, and Willard had all attended school there.

Upon further searching, Tyler had gone on to be a real estate agent and owned several rental houses and apartment buildings in the area. Presley Whitfield had worked as a maintenance man at Tyler's Real Estate Management Company.

Checking Whitfield's criminal record, found that Whitfield spent very little in jail – the charges being dismissed within days.

Marcia suspected Tyler had given Whitfield a place to live in one of the apartments – in exchange for doing some kind of work.

Willard Osmond had joined the Air Force and served four years in the states and Germany. Then he disappeared from view, as Marcia could not find another thing about him for the next five years.

Underground, she thought. *Probably dealing drugs and whatever else.*

So they were all in business, but the wrong business.

Marcia picked up the phone and called Richie.

"Got some good news," Marcia said.

"Oh?"

"Yes. Rufus saw the shadow man attend Tyler Harrisen's dinner at The Lighthouse Restaurant last night."

"That's interesting. Got a name?"

"Yes. Willard Osmond. Went to the Air Force for a few years, came back, and now lives on Juniper Street in one of Tyler's apartments."

Richie murmured and listened closely.

"Next door to the deceased, Presley Whitfield," she added.

"Wow. What else?"

"Rufus is having trouble with his min-camera, so he went out to buy a belt camera. Said his belly might be too big though."

"You put him on diet?"

"No. The problem is Sherry Linton's desserts. Rufus is over there every day at lunch feeding and cajoling her."

"Cajoling? Is that harassment?"

"No. That's strategic fraternalization."

"Wow. You detectives belong in the psychoanalytical field. We lawyers call that sexual harassment. You get a picture of that Osmond fellow?"

"He got a picture, and the man looks like the man who got out of that cab."

"So either there was a payoff or some conversation going on."

"Yes. Willard didn't go there for the chicken wings."

"How about Doebe? Margaret couldn't find much about him."

"He's not from around here. Came from Ohio and went to Medical School at Duke and landed here at the Medical Center via the General Hospital. I'll see if there have been any complaints against him at the Medical Board. Reckon who told him to plant Bobby Hutchings?"

They were both quiet for a few seconds over the phone.

Marcia spoke up and said, "Had to be Willard Osmond. Someone had some kind of power to get that done."

"But Willard Osmond will be gone."

164

Marcia thought about it for a second and knew Richie was probably right.

"I get Doebe on the stand and can bring Willard back to life," Richie said.

"Sounds like a plan. You give me life."

Richie smiled but said nothing, since he knew Marcia would answer him with wisdom he couldn't figure out.

He thanked her for all the research and said he'd see her later – it was about time they go fishing again.

She smiled and said, "I hope so."

"Send me a bill and Margaret will put a check in the mail."

"Okay darling."

25.

Richie Granger sat at his desk pondering the Hutchings' case.

He knew Jorge was getting pressure to prosecute Bobby Hutchings, if nothing but to hide the truth about what really happened.

But he would not wait for the rock to fall: he'd draft a Bill of Complaint against the state, since Rep. Harrisen was somehow involved. He'd list the facts of the case and relevant parties, and he would ask a prayer for relief and compensation – for the time Bobby had lost at work, home, and in life.

He might even ask the Board of Medicine to take away Doebe's license to practice medicine, but he knew Doebe was in contact with Jorge about something concerning the case; Margaret had heard something about it at lunch with courthouse workers.

The best scenario would be for the doctor to testify about the implant, if he was still alive.

Someone had funded the doctor's actions in Richie's mind. Threats aside, there was some motivation for the Doctor to do what he did.

Richie would need a diagnosis of the white spots in Bobby's X-ray, because there was something in Bobby's ear canal and upper neck, from what he could see on the film.

He would subpoena the Signal's analyst from Remote Tracking Service to talk about remote neural monitoring and tracking – along with the system's capability to coerce abnormal behavior.

But he would need to find out who, or what, gave Dr. Doebe motivation to implant Bobby Hutchings.

Willard would be gone, but the distributor of the device would not be.

Talk about product liability, he thought.

Richie decided to put these issues on hold for now. He had enough time to file a response with another week left of the thirty days Judge Burrow had mentioned. He would wait on Jorge's supposed charges.

When Richie came to work a couple of days later, there was a package on his desk from CARES – the non-profit company who was nice to enough to donate legal fees.

Margaret heard the unwrapping of paper through the doorway and said, "That package on your desk came late yesterday."

"Okay. Got it. Thanks," he said, as he laid his briefcase down on the chair and sat down to open the box's contents.

Inside were documents with C.I.A. letterheads and an Inspector General's report listing programs and subprojects of programs that detailed human behavior modifications and experiments on Native Americans and unwitting victims beginning in 1953 on the West

Coast of the United States with over 100 hospitals participating in the projects.

As he turned each of the pages, there was a list of medical centers that had participated in the programs -- funding apparatus – and substances that were used on the victims: drugs, radiation, or subcutaneous injections of composites.

Richie sat back in his chair thinking. *I'm suing the wrong people. I need to list the C.I.A. as a party. May have to find and bring in the Shadow Man after all.*

Richie made duplicate copies of the most relevant papers and put the originals in a safe.

He walked into the front office and asked Margaret to send the company a note of thanks.

"Good material?"

"Very good. Looks like we're in it for the long haul," Richie said, as he meandered back to his office and thought about another fishing trip.

Sure would be nice to find Osmond though, he thought.

He gave Marcia a call to see if she could help.

"Might," she said over the telephone. "I'll call the detective and see what's happening."

26.

Marcia picked up her office phone and left Captain Tellis a message about finding Willard Osmond.

Then she got up and walked closer to the window where Rufus was standing and looked at him sympathetically, "She working today?"

"I don't know. I was checking out the traffic."

"Yeah, and I'm looking for silver dollars on the sidewalk below."

"Tellis called earlier and wants to see you," Rufus said.

"I just called him and left a message."

"He's probably out of the office or busy. Just go over there."

"What does he want, you reckon?" Marcia asked.

"Don't know."

"Oh, yeah. Remember, he offered us jobs last year. Must be one open."

"Don't think that's it. He wants info."

"We got info."

"True. But I'm not as pretty as you."

"Shave and a haircut."

"But then I can't sleuth," Rufus said, as he turned away from the window. "Go see what he wants. Make a deal. Info for jobs, doughnuts, or something."

"Not something Rufus."

"Oh, forgot."

"Don't forget I'm a woman."

"No. Be careful. Jorge may behind it."

"Can't work two sides?"

"Not when you're in love with the defense attorney."

"Oh. Forgot about that. We both forget sometimes."

"Only when we should."

Marcia grabbed a notebook off her desk and told Rufus goodbye and not to worry about Sherry across the

171

street: she'd walk by the café window plenty of times for him to see.

Marcia walked the four blocks to the police station and up the second floor steps to look through a window to see Captain Tellis.

He motioned her in.

"How are you Marcia?"

"Doing well. Rufus sent me over here – said you wanted something."

"Have a seat."

Marcia walked over to a leather chair in front of the desk and sat down.

"What do you know about Willard Osmond?" he asked.

"Who wants to know?"

"I do. I'm the Chief of Police."

"And I'm Marcia Lane, private investigator who entertains private client privilege."

"He's your client?"

"No, but I've been hired by an attorney to find out certain things about who killed Presley Whitfield."

"Okay. What'll it be for info?"

"Rufus likes doughnuts."

"Doughnuts it is. Have them shipped over in the morning."

"The guy lives, or lived I should say, on Juniper Street, visits Langley quite often, and has a bad habit of disappearing."

"Got some of that. Where is he now?"

"Probably on an airplane."

"Going to where?"

"Don't know. Planes can fly thousands of miles in many directions, especially a Gulfstream or Dassault."

"Yes."

"But not private jets from Langley," Marcia said.

"Wow. You are good!"

"Rufus likes chocolate, and we'd like Willard Osmond back in the states."

"The chocolate doughnuts are no problem, but the fugitive is. What country is he in?"

"Germany's a good bet, since that name was on some of the papers Osmond had left behind in Bobby's cab. But two of the listed names on the papers had addresses in the Netherlands."

"Interpol may operate in those countries. I'll check on it."

"Anything else?"

"Not now, but thanks for coming over here."

"You will let us know, right?" Marcia asked before she stood up.

"Sure, sure. We'll let you know."

27.

Tellis called Martin Stocholm at the F.B.I.
Headquarters in Washington, D.C.

Martin saw the incoming phone number and knew it
was Tellis from Hampton, Virginia, from when the two
men had collaborated on a criminal case a year earlier
and put an end to drug running, stalking, and criminal
solicitation in the Hampton-Newport News area.

"Hey Chief," Martin said answering the phone.

"How'd you know?"

"Who could forget your number and the case there last year? How's the pretty girl? She involved in something again?"

"If you're talking about Marcia Lane, yes, that and more."

"Yes. The one who claimed she was cyber stalked and became a private investigator?"

"She just walked out of the office. That's her. She's been hired to investigate a murder -- came across an extortion and kidnapping operation – and one Willard Osmond who's been flying kids to other countries out of Langley A.F.B.."

"Wow! And what do you want us to do?"

"Find him. He's got some kind of connection to a murder victim and a doctor who targeted the killer."

"Wow, wow."

"It appears he has packed up and left the area. Marcia thinks he went overseas."

"And what would give her that idea?"

"She made a trip to Langley and acquired a flight manifest with the initials W.O. on it as the pilot of a plane that had left the airstrip early one morning. She located his private residence and found it emptied last week. A neighbor there told one of our investigators that Willard Osmond often bragged about having a chalet in Germany, where he visited every month. And Germany was one of two countries listed on a set of papers that were found by a cabbie in the back of the cab."

"What's the other country?"

"The Netherlands."

"We got connections with those two. Have a cause order signed by a judge and fax it to me with a request for extradition back to the U.S. to stand trial in a murder case."

"Okay. Got it. Thanks a lot."

"Hey. Would help if we knew what plane he was on."

"It was a private plane. She said something about a Gulfstream or Dassault."

"Well, that helps. The more information I have on the cause order, the better."

Martin said goodbye and went back to his computer tracking down a man on the F.B.I.'s list of most wanted people.

Tellis walked over to a clerk and asked her to get a cause order ready to get Osmond found and returned.

She pulled a blank order out from a folder, made a copy, put it in a word processer and typed Osmond's name on it. She laid it on an associate's desk and looked at him sternly and said, "Captain wants this signed by a judge ASAP."

The man walked over to the courthouse and found an on-duty judge who was sitting in his office reading a newspaper.

The judge looked the order over and signed it. The man walked back to the law enforcement building and faxed the order to the F.B.I.'s fax line. After a minute, the machine gave him a duplicate stating the copy had been delivered.

28.

After Stocholm received the judge's order, he faxed it to Interpol authorities in Germany.

Interpol police found Osmond's plane at Mannheim, after it had first landed at Frankfurt and been re-fueled. Retrieving registration records of the plane from the Internet and Frankfurt Airport, Osmond was found living at 27 Die Garten Park in Mannheim.

A policeman was dispatched and Osmond was taken away in handcuffs to a jail three blocks away.

He was kept there until Detective Brownlee arrived from the U.S. three days later.

Brownlee had flown to Frankfurt, transferred by small plane to Mannheim, and took a cab to the police station.

He walked in the station and introduced himself – showed his identification – and asked to see Osmond.

The consulate on duty led him down a hall to where there were four steel barred cells.

Osmond had an idea someone was coming to get him; otherwise, he would have had a scheduled hearing before a judge.

Osmond looked at Brownlee and said, "I didn't do it."

"You did something, or I wouldn't be here."

"But not murder," Osmond said as he looked through the side bar grills while the consulate was unlocking the door and readying some handcuffs.

"Well, then what?"

"I just roomed across from him."

"Roomed from across whom?"

Osmond shut up, wondering how much the police knew about his relationship with Whitfield and maybe even Representative Tyler Harrisen.

The detective checked the cuffs on Osmond's hands and took the keys back from the guard. He led Osmond to the front of the building where he signed a release form and thanked the officer for holding him.

Brownlee and Osmond stepped into a police van and were driven to Frankfurt; where they got on a U.S bound jet that took eight hours to fly to Washington D.C.

Brownlee led Osmond to a police car that had been waiting for them at the front entrance of the airport; they arrived in Hampton at 9:00 in the morning, where Osmond was put in jail.

When Captain Tellis saw Brownlee come in with Willard Osmond, a big smile came across his face.

But he wondered just how long an international criminal would stay under his jurisdiction; he walked over to Jorge's office and inquired.

"How long will Osmond be here?"

"Didn't know he was. But if he is, and I suppose you have custody of him, it would depend on what he is guilty of. We know he had something to do with the murder of Presley Whitfield and being in Bobby Hutchings' cab, from what Richie has said. But then, there's this manifest thing and some papers with private parties' names and personal information. Let's see what he does. He may want a lawyer, but then again, no lawyer may want to come out of the woodwork and expose himself as a friend of Osmond. Give it a couple days, and we'll see what happens. Probably will get a public defender to represent him."

"Okay, sounds good," Tellis said, and he returned to his desk still wondering.

Tellis wasn't through with his inquisition. If anyone would know more about what was happening, Marcia Lane would.

He called her and gave her the latest news about Osmond.

"Very good Captain. I'm glad it worked out," she said.

And she would say no more -- not wanting to speculate on something she wasn't sure about.

Tellis let it go and hung up.

But Marcia got on the phone and called Richie to tell him the news about Osmond being in jail.

"Great," he said.

Now, if he could only keep Osmond safe until he squealed on his bosses and gave away some information about why civilian passengers were getting on a plane out of Langley A.F.B.

A public defender, Jeri Sanchez, met with Osmond and told him he was looking at 15 years for being an accomplice in murdering Whitfield. Sanchez didn't have all the facts; she had only briefly looked at the file on record; she was mainly trying to scare him into talking about his activities surrounding his flights to Europe before she started defending him and becoming embarrassed.

One thing she knew was that Osmond had custody of those papers, and that Whitfield was a friend who lived across from him. That was enough for her to proclaim a pre-sentencing theory to get him to talk. She wanted to know what she was getting into.

But Osmond wouldn't talk.

Osmond's arrogance had got him off to a bad start.

The next day, after Richie had sent her a copy of the surveillance tape from Langley, and yearbook photos of

Osmond, Harrisen, and Whitfield together as friends --
she went ballistic.

In her next meeting with Osmond, she told him
things were changing by the hour: he was now looking
at 50 years for international trafficking, conspiracy to
commit murder, and bribery.

"I still ain't talking."

"Well, what are those sounds coming out of your
mouth? Gurgles? You can talk. You just aren't talking
about your criminal activities."

"Well. You know what will happen."

"I know what will happen if you don't talk. You'll
spend the rest of your life plus some in prison. And by
the way, the government has acquired a civil forfeiture
order on your assets."

"Not my personal goods!"

"You'll be lucky to keep any clothes on your back,
after all the expenses at Langley."

"What about my plane?"

"Oh, yes. Let's talk about the plane. Where did you
get the money to buy it?"

Osmond looked down at the tabletop and quieted
himself.

"Exactly. Drug money. And we could delve a little deeper into someone funding Representative Harrisen's campaign."

Osmond's eyes lightened up with concern. "I can't talk. They'll kill me if I talk."

"You're going to die anyway, and better than rotting in prison with a guilty conscience."

And with that, Jeri gathered her briefcase and umbrella on that rainy day and walked out of the Hampton Jail complex.

29.

A couple of weeks passed and Jorge Melindez went to the courthouse and re-filed a charge of murder against Bobby Hutchings.

In two more weeks, Richie Granger filed a countersuit – stating the Bobby Hutchings was coerced by remote neural monitoring and the manipulation of magnetic fields by a computer programmer into killing Presley Whitfield.

Richie had enough evidence to prove his case --- to show a jury that Bobby was being influenced by an unseen source – one he hoped that Tomas Stillwell of Remote Tracking Services could substantiate and that Dr. Doebe would admit to being a party.

Doebe's confession would not come easy, but he had acknowledged the subpoena and planned to be at court.

His presence would not come without a cost: Dr. Doebe insisted he be exonerated from any wrong or criminal penalty if he confessed. The state granted him the request at the urging of Richie.

On the first day of jury selection, there were few spectators in the court. Hutchings and Whitfield had no relatives in the area since they were both former soldiers who were sent to and stationed at Fort Eustis.

Local people in the area felt the case was just another prosecution of man who was crazy and killed another man over a drug deal, from the conversations Richie had overheard in local diners.

But there were a few strange faces in the courtroom – people Richie had never seen at the first trial or around town – and they weren't there on a pleasure trip – wearing suits and ties. Neither did they look like notebook journalists looking for stories.

Marcia decided to stay away from the jury selection process – she wanted to be inconspicuous as possible. For one thing, she was concerned about her safety after meddling around Langley AFB, the cab company, and the apartments where Whitfield and Osmond had lived.

And she had a security guard job contract to fulfill three days a week at night with a construction company.

"Good money," Rufus had said, "for sitting in a vehicle looking at three pieces of heavy equipment on a newly developed housing project plot of land."

A backhoe had been stolen recently, so Rufus and Marcia were hired to watch the area.

But in the back of her mind, she wanted to see Hutchings freed and out of jail, and she still wondered just what kind of injections someone had put in him.

30.

Richie Granger now had some help: the court assigned an associate attorney to help with the case.

Renton Collier had just finished law school and was working in the public defender's office, when he was assigned to help Richie.

Renton showed up for trial a little disheveled with his black wavy hair falling in several directions: he had on a blue striped tie, tan polyester coat that was too short for his arms, and black cotton pants that looked as if they could have used some ironing.

Nevertheless, here he was in the courtroom with his notepad, pen, and a briefcase.

Selecting jurors by Richie had proved to be an easy process in the first trial – looking for people who would have compassion on Bobby as a poor cab driver who was minding his own business but harassed and targeted.

These new prospective jurors were settled in three rows opposite the jurors' box area, and Richie asked some standard questions about whether the person knew the defendant or the deceased; whether the person ever rode in Bobby's cab; and if the person had ever worked at Langley AFB.

Richie knew the people he wanted: young educated adults who had skills in computer management and software. They would understand the advances in technology that could be used to track a person -- and influence one's thoughts and actions with modulated energies to the nervous system.

Richie got the six people he wanted.

Jorge accepted six jurors who were older – people he thought would think Richie's argument of remote neural monitoring was hogwash.

And so trial began on the third day, with the jurors sitting in the jury box and the lawyers nervously adjusting their ties and loosening their coats.

The courtroom was filled with about thirty people and all rose when the bailiff announced the judge was entering the room.

Judge Burrow came in through a back door and sat down in the big black swivel chair behind the front podium: he put a file of papers off to the side.

He lightly tapped the gavel to the desk and looked to see if all the parties were rightly present.

Looking at Richie's assistant however; he smirked a little at the youngster's face and remembered when he tried his first case out of law school – sitting in front of Judge Harkins wondering when the judge would tell him to shut up after lengthy orations defending a client who been bit by a dog on a leash, but none came, and the old judge would come to treat him with respect and dignity.

A side door opened and Bobby Hutchings was escorted to a chair at the defendant's table – beside Richie – who had already discussed the new trial procedures with Bobby four days ago in the prison visiting room.

Judge Burrow stretched out a few papers before him, shifted in his chair, and looked around the courtroom once more at the crowd: the last thing he needed was for someone to disrupt the proceedings.

He saw a policeman at the back door, and another one at the front side door. The transcriber was sitting down at a desk a few feet from the juror's box.

And all the jurors were there.

When conversational chatter in the room quieted, the judge announced why the case was taking place, and he gave Jorge Melindez the floor to speak.

Jorge walked around his table to the front of the courtroom and faced the jury.

He told the jury this was a simple case of murder – that Bobby Hutchings purposely killed Whitfield because he was paranoid about someone coming into his apartment and harassing him: the police had Bobby's gun, the bullet casings matched the shells in Whitfield's body, and Bobby admitted to doing it.

Unwisely, he told the court about Richie's pre-conceived argument – about some crazy in outer space directing all this activity.

Jorge kept his talk short and sat back down in his chair.

Richie Granger rose from his table in a carefree manner knowing that he was treading in uncharted territory: no one in the United States had brought such a controversial argument to any court – that blamed a murder on the use of technology.

But here he was, about to show the jury and spectators that a sinister computer programmer somewhere was behind the murder, which in essence, was happening throughout the country with the amount of unexplained killings and violence.

Richie would use an allegory of two men.

"Two men became acquainted with each other in a coffee shop. Within minutes, after having a light breakfast, they walked out the door and down a sidewalk, one behind the other for a couple minutes. The second man looked ahead of him and saw a gold coin on the walkway, and he thought the fellow ahead might have dropped it. But the fellow was long gone, so the man took it home and hid it. Several hours later, the man who lost the coin figured it to be on that sidewalk where he had pulled a handkerchief from his pocket. But when he went back to look for it, it was not there – and he remembered the other man following him. The man wanted his coin back, just as the man, in this case, Willard Osmond, wanted his papers back -- papers that contained addresses, phone numbers, and other personal information of private citizens – including credit card numbers and personal identification numbers. Worse, there were kids' names on these papers, and some kind of codes of genetic descent."

Richie walked over to his table and lifted the papers high for the people to see.

"Within a couple of days, Bobby Hutchings' apartment was broken into and rummaged. That failing, Bobby woke up one morning weeks later to find blood on his pillow, and the apartment door unlocked. Someone had been in his apartment and done something to him. Bobby starts to have pain in his ears and head. He goes to a doctor, who gives him medicine, but Bobby begins to have nightmares and illusions – goes back to the doctor, and the doctor performs minor surgery. To

Bobby's disdain, the doctor has placed a mini-receiver in Bobby's ear area."

The jurors had looked bored until Richie made that statement, but slowly, one by one, a head raised up in expectation something important was really about to happen in the trial.

Richie paused a couple of seconds to give the jurors time to think about what he had just said, then he continued: "The evidence will show that Bobby was coerced by technology into killing Presley Whitfield. If Presley did not die, he would have confessed that Osmond, the man who lost the papers, was a racketeer and working for the C.I.A. The two men lived next to each other in an apartment building."

Richie paused and let than sink into the jury.

"The evidence will also show that remote targeting of a person's actions and thoughts can be accomplished with a computer program and micro-chip, which in this case, to a micro-chip that had been placed in Bobby's head by Dr. Doebe. Not to get too far off the subject, one might ask what motivated the doctor to perform such a procedure."

Richie walked back to the table and traded papers and held them high.

"These right here. They give doctors permission to experiment on people with microchips by a grant from the Virginia Department of Health through the Department of Human and Health Services of the U.S. Government. Coincidentally, covert activity of this type has been taking place by the Government since 1953 upon Native Americans, and Bobby is Cherokee. In this case, Dr. Doebe, who was Bobby's doctor, received one of these grants and devices. Be reminded that non-consensual experimentation, or a patient who did not authorize medical treatment, violates the law. Bobby did not authorize the implantation: he was there to get his ears drained. Bobby was harassed, targeted, and was wittingly used by cyber targeting to kill Presley Whitfield to save Willard Osmond's racketeering enterprise that was taking place from a government installation. I would ask the jury to find Bobby Hutchings not guilty."

31.

It was eerily quiet after Richie had finished his opening statement.

The bailiff's hard shoe soles could be heard scraping the floor as he nervously walked to a side door and looked through its reinforced window.

A few people turned their heads to look at him.

He turned his head back quickly to the podium and walked back to his original place of standing. He wiped his forehead with a handkerchief, as Judge Burrow looked towards him curiously.

Other than that, there was the slight rumbling of the air conditioning fan motor from overhead reverberating throughout the courtroom.

Jorge sat silently, tapping his pen on the table and looking over the list of witnesses.

But Starling Meeks, Bobby's girlfriend, was about to produce a whole new atmosphere in the courtroom when she pressed the call button on her cell phone that she had sneaked by the door guard – to alert a leader of seven bystanders from the CARES organization who were mingling in the hallway just outside the courtroom.

When the call came, the organizer nodded her head to the other participants, and each person took a sign from beneath their shirts and extended a stick with a sign that said "Free Bobby Hutchings". They began marching in a circle crying out, "Justice for Bobby Hutchings, Justice for Bobby Hutchings".

Starling sat silently wondering if her plan had worked, but when she heard the commotion and the chanting outside the room, she smiled and bowed her head. She considered the mission accomplished and glad she wasn't in the hallway.

It took the bailiff thirty seconds to get to the front door and usher the group to the exterior of the building while calling for help on his shoulder radio.

Richie was still sitting down but welcomed the commotion -- which would give the jury more time to think about his opening statement.

Jorge waited for the commotion to settle and then called Detective Brownlee to testify about the statements Bobby had made in an interrogation room after the murder -- the fact that Bobby owned the murder weapon – and that a ballistics expert had matched the shell in Presley Whitfield's dead rib cage.

On cross-examination, Richie asked the detective if there was another man in the apartment enclave. The detective said he had no evidence there was another man: there were no security cameras in the vicinity. But he did say that Bobby had said there was another man.

Bobby Hutchings sat at the defendant's table in his orange jumpsuit looking rather spiffy – like he had just come out of a shower. His hair was neatly combed back and he had a fresh shave.

He was happy the truth was coming out about the remote targeting issue: he had been trying to get people to listen to him for a month -- and now this lawyer, Richie Granger, was arguing his case – with funding from an Indian rights organization Bobby had contacted earlier.

Bobby wondered about all the other inmates in jails throughout the country who had been victims of remote targeting, and committed crimes. Maybe his case would pave the way for them to become acquitted of the crimes committed. *And wouldn't it be great if a conspirator to the targeting confessed about such innocuous activities?*

Jorge had followed through with a threat to shut down the case based upon remote technology being used as some kind of a state secret that protected the nation, but Judge Burrow would have none of it and denied the motion. The judge had enough of these cases on the docket, and he wanted the truth out about this human targeting issue.

Starling did not want to testify as a character witness for Bobby, but at the last minute, she agreed to take the stand if called.

Fred Fulton was glad to come to trial and talk about Bobby: he wanted Bobby back to work.

Bobby had always reported on time to work, had his mileage meter and fees matched with pick-ups and let-offs, and kept his cab clean when he came back to the shop at nights.

Richie put Fred on the stand and got his testimony, though some of it was damaging to his case when Fred said Bobby was not the same person after the Memorial Day weekend.

Richie asked him, "What do you mean, he wasn't the same person?"

"Well, he couldn't remember directions to a couple of places, and I had to help him. Another time, a regular customer called and said Bobby had called her by the wrong name, though he knew her well. And then the money was off by $10.00 one night, which had never happened."

Richie could only interject, "Well, this all happened after he had possession of those papers and was being harassed by Presley Whitfield."

Jorge quickly stood up and said, "I object Your Honor. He hasn't stated exact dates of such incidents, and there's no proof of when Hutchings started acting erratically."

"Sustained. Are you through with the witness, counsel?"

Richie felt flushed for a moment, because he was unable to come up with exact dates. Maybe it was because of the stress or he didn't remember, so he told the judge yes and released Fred Fulton from the stand.

With that, Judge Burrow released the jury and the attorneys for lunch.

32.

Richie slowly walked back to his table and gathered his files. He asked Renton if he would like to go to lunch somewhere but Renton said no -- he was still grabbled by events of the last hour and trying to figure things out.

Richie saw his puzzled face and said, "Don't worry. It will all work out. This trial is just a little different than most."

Renton nodded his head and said, "Okay, Mr. Granger. Whatever you say. I'll just stay here and try to set a schedule for the afternoon's agenda."

"Fine, fine."

Richie saw that all of the people in the seats had left. *No sense in staying in a courtroom if a person didn't have to,* he thought.

He walked out of the courthouse confident he had done a good job. He didn't see any of the demonstrators or protests going on outside.

It was a pretty day in August, and he thought the fish may be plentiful, as they would be heading out of the bay migrating south.

A man, who had a ponytail with a turquoise leather barrette, approached him as he walked down a long tree-lined walkway towards the courthouse café.

"Richie Granger?" he said.

"Yes."

"Won't take up much of your time. I'm Jim Cloudwaters, partner with the CARES group and funding your representation of Bobby Hutchings."

"Oh, yes. Pleased to meet you," Richie said as he reached to shake his hand.

Jim was dressed in a sleeveless leather shirt with tassels hanging from the pockets and forest green canvas pants with pockets just above the knees on both sides.

He wore tan moccasins – and a black onyx stone set in tarnished gold hung around his neck.

"Can we sit and talk somewhere?" he asked.

"I was just going to lunch. You're welcome to join me for twenty minutes or so."

"That should do it."

They both walked to the café and sat down in a booth that was sectioned off from other seats. A waitress came over and both men ordered a glass of water and some French fries with onion rings.

"How's it going over there?" Jim asked.

"All well, considering. The courthouse hasn't blown up and all parties are present."

Jim smiled a little and thought this case could truly change the destiny of his American Indian nation and grant them immunity from the white man's power aggression over nature and the people. Water on many Reservations was being poisoned from large factories upstream, and politics were keeping the Indians oppressed and targeted, especially with the surveillance methods.

"These things, the rich and powerful do, in the name of progression, are destroying our people," Jim said.

"I know."

"For years, they enter our lands and stick our people with needles, force hard pills into our mouths, and now we have to listen to music and subliminal voices through the airwaves that are not from our heavenly Father on earth or the heavens."

"I have heard of these things," Richie said in his most Indian monotone.

"I want to thank you for representing Bobby. He was a young boy on our Reservation who knows the old way. If there is no way out for him, can you try and get him near home where we can take care of him?"

Richie wanted to keep this conversation short: he had enough on his mind with an afternoon's session in court without getting into a dialogue of Indian descendent rights and cultural disseminations in a modern day of life and technology and government overload.

"I will try," he responded.

After sitting awhile longer and talking about sports, the military, and trial procedures, Richie said bye and dropped a $10.00 bill on the table and walked out of the café.

Jim finished eating the last of the fries and drank some water while musing over the meeting.

Nice man that Richie, he thought as he looked at the money on the table and the empty basket of fries.

33.

When Richie arrived back at the courthouse and settled into his seat, he looked back at the crowd and saw some different faces.

A few were middle-aged men with black and white uniforms. Richie figured them to be friends from Fred's Cab Company.

After the judge entered the room and rendered that all parties were present, including the jurors, Richie called Doctor Doebe to the stand and the clerk swore him in.

Jorge knew the doctor had agreed to come, but it was only after receiving a promise of immunity from the state that Richie would be able to question him.

When Doebe had received the subpoena, he knew his medical career was over if he talked about implanting Bobby Hutchings with an electronic receiver, but to hide his action was something he did not want to live with the rest of his life – especially knowing it contributed to a man being killed.

He first contacted an acquaintance at the State Medical Board and told him the story.

The friend had said, "Doebe, You got three choices: you can fight this issue for six months and probably get a suspension of five years; you can try to come to an agreement with the victim and pay an unlimited amount of money and get the insurance company mad at you; or you can quit and be hounded the rest of your life."

Doebe chose the hounds. He contacted his lawyer and told him the story. The lawyer drew up a declaration of immunity and got it signed by a judge in agreement with the state.

So he decided to testify about the implant, hurry out of court and town, and find a new job.

Sure, he had received a life threatening phone call from an unknown person and being nearly run off the road while he was driving one day, but his integrity here was at stake, and that was something he wanted to keep.

Doebe was dressed in a black suit with a blue and red striped tie. He sat and relaxed in the chair next to the judge's podium.

Richie walked over to him and asked some standard questions about how long the doctor had been practicing medicine, how long had he been treating Bobby Hutchings, and the location of his work areas.

The doctor answered each question, and Jorge Melindez did not object to any answer -- until Richie asked Dr. Doebe about neurological implants and the effects on an individual.

"Your Honor," Jorge said. "The man is an Ear, Nose, and Throat Doctor. The question is irrelevant to his practice. "

Richie didn't give Judge Burrow time to glance towards him for a response and said, "Ear, nose, and throat doctors work with nerves every day. It's more than relevant, considering Bobby Hutchings X-Rays show a subcutaneous device in his ear canal that contributed to behavior modification. The man went to Medical School for eight years."

Judge Burrow said, "The defendant has charged the state with technological coercion and the doctor is well qualified to speak on any matter concerning the head area: I'll allow the question but get to the point quick about how it is relevant to the case."

Turning towards Dr. Doebe, Richie asked him, "According to the records Doctor, you treated Bobby twice with anti-biotics and gave him a prescription for some ear drops. But what did you do the third time?"

"First, I cleaned his ear canals out with an anti-septic solution, but there is some thought in the medical field that a mini-receiver could stimulate the canal to produce certain antibodies to fight off infection and clear the area for standard hearing."

"And did you insert this device?"

"I was encouraged to."

"Who encouraged you to?"

"Not only the F.D.A., who had supplied me with such a device, but a middle aged man came through my office doors before Bobby Hutchings' appointment and told me that if I did not implant the patient – my license to practice medicine would be terminated."

"Who was this man?"

"I don't know, but he was serious and I believed him."

"Can you can describe him?"

"Yes."

"Is he in this courtroom?"

"No."

"And you went ahead with the procedure?"

"Yes. A ten millimeter micro-chip was placed near ear canal area with a microscopic antenna -- and two injections in the neck area which if activated facilitate voice modulation to the brain."

The 12 jurors sat spellbound as Richie looked towards them to gauge their reactions.

Richie didn't expect the doctor to be so truthful about the operation, but here it was in front of the jury and the people; so he quieted himself, expecting a harsh response from Jorge who sat stone faced and was twiddling a pen on the top of the table. Jorge had enough of his own mind-controlled victims' cases on his desk to know the doctor was telling the truth.

Everything in the courtroom got real quiet as the doctor looked from the stand and stared straight ahead; he looked as if he wanted to talk more but kept silent.

Richie didn't know else what to ask, sensing this testimony alone was strong enough to convince the jury that silent sound technology to a person's head was real.

So Richie stopped, backed up a few steps, thanked the doctor, and said there were no more questions.

Jorge had a couple however, and he stood up quickly to address the doctor.

"Doctor Doebe. Was this device you are talking about F.D.A. approved?"

"Yes. Well, I don't really know."

"Well, either it is or it isn't. Was there an information packet with the device that had instructions and the date of its manufacture and origin?"

"I don't know counselor. The pack was sent to me from a medical supply company a week earlier in generic packaging. There were instructions on how to use its contents. The F.D.A. had sent out information about such a packet in a memorandum a month earlier."

Jorge had no idea what to ask next, so he released the doctor from any further questioning.

Richie then called Robert Trane to the stand. Robert was the X-Ray technician with the medical center who had taken X-Rays of Bobby's head.

Richie had him state his name, place of work, and job experience. There were no objections because Jorge had the man's information in the file and saw nothing amiss.

Richie walked over to his table and retrieved a darkened envelope with film copies of the X-Rays. He walked over to Mr. Trane and handed it to him.

"Mr. Trane, Are these the X-Rays you took of Bobby's head?"

Mr. Trane looked at the identification number and date at the bottom of the copies and affirmed it was.

Richie gave him a few more seconds to look at the films and asked, "What is the brighter spot above the right ear?"

"It's an unknown object about ½" in length and 1/16" in diameter."

"Could it be a microscopic antenna?"

"I don't know what that is."

"Objection Your Honor. Counsel is speculating. The point has been made something is there," Jorge said.

"Sustained. Get on with it."

Richie turned towards Mr. Trane. "Okay, you don't know what it is, but it is something that is not likely to be there in a normal process of growth."

"Correct."

"That's all I have," Richie said, and he went to his table.

Jorge arose and asked Mr. Trane, "Have you seen anything like this before on an X-Ray?"

"Well, several times."

"Explain that please."

"Bullet fragments, needle perforations, or injury substances look similar."

"Thank you Mr. Trane. You may step down," he said, as he looked at Richie who had his head bowed looking through another file folder.

Richie called the Signal's Analyst from Remote Tracking Services, Mr. Tomas Stillwell, to the stand and asked him specific questions about technology being able to control a person with microwaves, electro-magnetic energy, or radio frequencies.

The technician affirmed there were patents on such propagating devices and explained that he had recorded pulsed modulated voice synthetic signals to Bobby's head with a listen-up device and recorder.

"Can you explain this in simpler terms to a person who has no knowledge about such media?"

"Well, I'll try. Everyone has a distinct bio-electric signal that can be monitored and influenced. In Bobby's case, I used a spectrum analyzer in a radio free area to find signals that were not in the immediate electromagnetic spectrum hearing area. Once I found several abstract signals with a scanner, I focused on one that was cycling above 20,000 hertz in the ultrasonic range, which could affect a person's thoughts and behavior. The listen-up device also picked up secondary recorded transmissions that were violent, including instructing the victim, in this case Bobby Hutchings, to murder a man. The N.S.A., C.I.A., and the Defense Department are aware of this technology."

Just about the time Tomas Stillwell had finished his statement, a turbo-charged jet flew slowly over the courthouse making a horrific sound that made the courthouse shake and sound echoing off the plastered walls.

People in the courtroom seats looked around with wonder, while jurors' eyelids opened wider and stared at the lawyers.

When everything was calm, Richie asked, "What would give a person the authority to use such artificial voice technology to the head of person?"

"There's no such authority to harm a person with electronic signals. Signals being used for purposes other than what they were designed for in communications are illegal."

Jorge again stood and objected: "Your Honor. There is no precedent for that issue and I ask the remark be stricken from the record."

"Agreed. The jury will ignore the remark."

"Okay, Tomas. Are you aware of the patents of such technology?"

"Patents have been registered for the technology since the early 1990's. Anyone with the right equipment such as a silent sound recorder hooked up with an FM signal, television station, or some kind of target could easily send these transmissions to or near an individual and make that individual think they are hearing their own words."

"Thank you Mr. Stillwell."

Jorge Melindez got up from his chair, walked to the middle of the front of the courtroom, and turned towards Mr. Stillwell.

"Mr. Stillwell. Could anyone have whispered into your listen-up device and conveyed the instructions you are talking about?"

"Could but no. The device operates on a separate frequency than that of the human voice. It modulates the voice into a radiological frequency from the sender to the receiver."

"Okay. How many people have you tested for this technology?"

"Several."

"And they all murdered someone?"

"No, no. They were being labeled as mentally ill and wanted to prove that they were being targeted by a remote artificial device."

"And were your tests successful?"

"Very much so, such that each person would be released from psychiatric care and psychotropic drugs to lead a somewhat normal life."

"Why couldn't a person lead a normal life?"

"In many subjects, synthetic receivers in the form of sodium transmitters, micro-chips, or carbonized particles have been injected into the victims' heads and organs that interrupts the thought process. Removal of such media could endanger a person's neurological functions for life, and may even cause death. Implants cannot always be removed from a person due to their proximity to blood veins, nerve centers, or critical organs."

"I see. Do you have practical experience in the medical field about such incidents?"

"Don't need it. Two of the victims who tried the procedure ended up dying on the operating table according to a study done by doctors in the Simon Neurological Institute in Amsterdam."

"That's all I have," Jorge said.

Judge Burrow excused Mr. Stillwell from the witness box and tapped his gavel to the desk. He told the people that court was adjourned for the day, and he told the jurors to report back at 9:00 in the morning.

Richie was ecstatic he had got the witnesses to talk about remote neural monitoring.

And so far, no one had done anything to disrupt the trial – other than the overhead jet and the CARES group.

34.

While trial was taking place, Marcia was sitting at her desk in her office when a man opened the door and made his way in as if he owned the place. Another fellow followed, and stood against the wall with his arms crossed.

The first man, who had entered the room, looked at Marcia, and said, "You Marcia Lane?"

"That depends on who you are and why you don't have enough manners to knock on the door," Marcia said, as she sat back in her chair and sized the situation up.

"Ain't got time for chit-chat."

"You've come to the right place: there is no chit and chat here. Try downstairs at the furniture store."

"Look lady. You and your attorney boyfriend are treading in dangerous territory and need to stop."

"It's a free country big mouth. Now you have one minute to exit the building or I'm pushing this little button here to send in the police," Marcia said as she pointed to a phone on the desk.

"Hold on lady. Let's talk."

"We can start by you introducing you and your partner."

"I'm Nort and that's Red."

"Who sent you to threaten me?"

"Lay off Osmond and we'll tell you who sent us."

"Osmond is a racketeer, and a big one at that."

"Where is he?"

"Why you want to know?"

"Boss wants to know."

"Boss who?"

Nort looked at Red and Red shook his head from side to side.

"Babysit him or something?" Marcia asked.

"Osmond shortchanged him on some fees."

"Let me guess. Osmond pimps girls in your neighborhood without you getting a boarding fee."

"Something like that. Now where is he?"

"I don't know. Looking for him myself," Marcia lied.

Nort stood motionless and looked around the office. Red dropped his arms and put his hands in his pockets.

"What now?" Red said as he looked at Nort.

"We wait. We know you're looking for him, probably for that court case. But then he goes to jail and the boss is still out, and he don't like that."

"Yea, well I don't like it either, but that's the way it goes sometimes. Now if you will kindly step outside and make your way down the stairs, there won't be any more time chit and chatting. Tell boss to keep his neighborhood a little more under control."

"I'll tell him, but he don't like anything about this court case you all are starting."

"Didn't start it. Presley Whitfield started it when he harassed Bobby Hutchings."

Nort turned around and walked through the door while Red followed him.

Marcia took her other hand off a gun under her desk and relaxed a little.

So this is what the detective business is really about, she thought. *People looking for people and threatening others. Still beats sitting at a desk and typing all day long. Boy, Rufus is going to love this.*

35.

Rufus showed up at the office just after lunch – after confirming Rep. Harrisen had gone to a town meeting in Hampton and told lies about what he could do for the people in the future, like replacing sand at the beach, making schools safer, and reducing crime.

Like many new politicians, the representative didn't understand the process of getting things done in government affairs: committee meetings, studies, comments from the public, and resolutions to the assembly that could be argued over for months.

Marcia was grateful for Rufus. Being tough and acting tough was not her game, but this investigating business demanded such traits when devils such as Nort and Red came around with bad manners.

She was calming down somewhat as her hands stopped shaking; she had been praying to God continuously after the two men had left.

However, the imprint from her sweaty hand was still on the desk from holding the gun so tight.

She sat back quickly and relaxed when he entered the door.

"Hi Rufus. How was your morning with the Rep.?"

Rufus looked at her quizzically and measured her unusual greeting.

"Okay. Same lies by another politician looking to gain popularity and enhance low self-esteem. What's up with you? Look like you've seen a ghost."

"That evident, huh? Two guys came in here and threatened me – said for me to get off the Hutchings' case and Osmond."

"Fantastic. Those are probably Baily's men," Rufus said as he took off his coat and settled in at his desk area.

"Excuse me?"

"Baily's men. Runs the west side crime sector. Does a little prostitution for the soldiers, a few drugs, and peddles some black market items at the stores. He's usually not a problem unless someone steps in his territory. They say what they want?"

"Says the boss wants Osmond – for some kind of tapping fee."

"Great. He send King Nort and Red?"

"Did. The guy who did all the talking was big and fat and said his name was Nort. The other guy was Red."

"Yep. That's them. They're not much of a problem if we give them something in return. What'd you tell them?"

"I told them to get out of the office or I was going to have some friends show up quickly."

"That'll do it," Rufus said as he shuffled some papers on his desk and looked at the clock on the wall.

"I told them that I didn't know where he was, and they walked out the door somewhat satisfied."

Rufus took a deep breath and ran his hand through his hair, while he looked through some mail on his desk.

"Well, they ain't going to be satisfied. I got an idea; since Osmond is in jail, tell them he owns a 2021 Audi sitting in the parking lot at his vacated residence."

"Good idea Rufus. We just want them off the case."

"Right. He gets his money and we carry on and stipulate they owe us a favor."

Changing the subject, Rufus asked, "Where we at on the case anyway?"

"The trial is in progress, but Richie hired us to find out who harassed Bobby Hutchings. Then some human rights organization got involved and started sending Richie money to find out if Bobby had reacted to some kind of remote energy targeting and the killing of Presley Whitfield, which led us to conduct more work and investigate Dr. Doebe -- the guy who was treating Bobby for ear problems. But to find the file Hutchings had discovered in the back of his cab, we had to check out Bobby's boss at the cab company, track down the unknown passenger in the cab, and find Remote Tracking Services to meet a technician and gather more paperwork about it all. We're up to 150 hours. "

"Cool."

Rufus sat back and thought about it: *Gee, that's $7,500 plus some travel and administrative costs for a couple of weeks work. Not bad.*

"Well, what's left to do?"

"Oh, we could do a lot more on this since he's got funding."

"Yeah, like using some money to buy our caskets and cemetery plots if we keep on."

"Well. There is that."

"Give it a little time and see how it goes. Baily though is something else. What would be the harm in us telling him that Osmond is in jail?" Rufus asked.

"None, as he long as gets killed in jail."

"That would give him something to think about. Well, give him something. Tell him about the car. I like to stay on good terms with the goons. Sometimes, they come in useful."

"I'll slip him the address where Osmond lived."

"That will help. And tell them they can have the car."

"Ha. We're in the car business now!"

"Only when they're condemned, and the owner is condemned."

"Perfect. You reckon the car is still there?"

"Is unless the feds got it. But they usually take thirty days to find a bathroom. Baily will get it one way or another. He's in the towing business too."

"Perfect. Where do I get in touch with godfather?"

"Club Diamond on Sandstone Road in the Flats in the afternoon. Don't go loaded."

"How about unloaded?"

"Should work, but they still may frisk you."

"Over my dead body."

"Right."

"Thanks Rufus."

"I'm closing this Harrisen job. There's nothing outstanding as criminal: it's not against the law to talk to someone on the way to the bathroom."

"No, it's not."

Check with Tellis and Richie occasionally and see what's happening in court. May be some more work there but don't stir a pot of boiling noodles."

"Sherry Linton across the street do that?"

"No. My little sister would though, and hot water usually came out onto the floor."

"I think I understand Rufus. Time for an ice cream and a milkshake. And oh, Tellis said doughnuts will be here in the morning."

"Awesome."

"Okay. I'm out of here."

"Where are you going?"

"To the Diamond Club like we talked about."

"You can't go by yourself. I'll call Starks."

"Who is Starks?"

"My strongman, 220 pounds of lean muscle skilled in judo and marksmanship."

"Wow! And I thought you were in this business alone."

"Every good Private Investigator has a back-up."

"Well, I got a back-up Rufus, higher than Stark. So don't worry. After I deliver this message to Baily, I'm heading over to see the CARES group people – see if they got more money."

"Now that's an idea. Where they at?"

"Jamestown, according to their card that Margaret gave me."

"Well, don't get scalped."

"You don't like my hair, do you?" Marcia said as she gathered her belonging and went to the door.

"Have a nice trip."

36.

Walking out to her car in the parking lot, Marcia took a notepad from her pocket and wrote down the former address of Willard Osmond and the make of his car. She folded it in half and stuck it in her pocket.

She drove to the Diamond Club and parked the car just inside an alley off the main road.

There was one door visible with a sign above the top, and when she knocked on it, Nort slowly opened it and stared at her.

She handed the note to him and said, "Rufus says you owe him one."

She quickly retracted her steps, got into the car, and took off to Jamestown.

Marcia found the address for the CARES group and parked her car on a two-car pebble-stoned driveway lined with railroad ties.

She got out and looked at a crudely constructed shack that had a wooden slat door and no visible windows – other than a shuttered opening.

A sign labeled "CARES" hung loosely on a small pole off to the side of a rock walkway.

She knocked on the wooden door, and in a few seconds, it slowly creaked open. An older Indian woman stood there in an indigo colored flowered dress with a light blue bandana tightly wrapped around her head.

The old lady raised her head slowly and looked at Marcia suspiciously, and said, "No. We don't want none."

"Oh, no. I'm not here to sell you anything. I want information."

"Information comes from the Holy Father," she said as she pointed to the sky. Do you not know?"

"Please, please. Let us talk and tell me more."

Emma Buckthorn looked on for curiously but didn't see anything wrong with inviting her in.

"Come in then."

Marcia walked into the single room shack and onto a rock floor that had been grouted with lime and chipped oyster shells. The walls of the house were pine boards with cement-filled gaps. In the corner of the room, sat a black wood stove, with a smoke pipe that extended out a sidewall. There was one opening, a wood shuttered window that was half-open with a little screening pushed into it.

The room smelled musty but comfortable, with an apple-scented candle burning on a counter.

"You live here?"

"No. This is the office."

Marcia smiled.

"We live over there," Emma said pointing to the James River a few hundred yards away.

She moved gracefully to the counter and lifted a cup of hot water off a small propane camp grill; then she went and sat down on a chair that had oak splits woven from side to side, with her dress hanging over the sides.

235

She looked up at Marcia, while cradling the warm dark brown ceramic cup of tea in her hands.

"Where we've always lived," she said, as her dark brown eyes looked at Marcia reflecting the image of a tired soul yet magnificently full of light and wisdom.

Marcia felt the earth momentarily stop. She felt like she had been transported back in time 600 years when the Spanish and English first arrived on shore and took many Indians as slaves and others as guides. Others they would prod and beg for food, and understanding about how to hunt and fish.

And so she was humbled -- and went to sit on a two-seat wooden bench at the backside of the room shaking just a little.

She crossed her legs and sat up straight with curiosity flowing out of her mind.

"Well, it's a beautiful area and you have survived."

"No. We have not survived. We are oppressed -- stricken with diseases unbeknownst to us."

Marcia felt a pang of guilt that she had not done something in the past to protect the rights of this "indigenous people" – as one encyclopedia described the Indians.

The old woman turned her head and looked out the front door across a gravel road to a telephone pole.

"Over there. Those wires in the sky. We thought they were traps for birds, but there are no nets."

Marcia smiled.

"Big cans are in the river, with lights that blink, but they are not stars. Rather than ride the tide, your people have big canoes that make hard sounds and drive the fish away. The birds are scared, and now the people. The big hard frames that are built towards the heavens have no eagles at the top."

Marcia shed a tear or two and said "Yes."

"Go talk with Jim Cloudwaters. He will tell you."

"Yes. Yes. I'll do that."

Marcia was deeply affected by each word the old lady spoke, and she bowed her head and felt remorse covering her soul and words.

She got up quietly from the bench and walked over to the counter where she had seen a business card. She nodded at Emma to see if it was okay if she got one, and Emma nodded yes.

Marcia said goodbye and walked out of the building feeling sad.

Later that evening, she called Jim Cloudwaters and talked about meeting Emma.

"Emma is not full of words: she is full of grief. At her age, she has seen devastation take place along the river. Land clearing, dredging the river, and smoke that is black and falls from the sky is ruining the earth."

"She told me a few of her complaints," Marcia said.

"What she says is true. The Indians are much oppressed. Their way of living has been destroyed. Horrific things have been done to them. The whites have tried to make them feel special, but behind their backs, and in the shadows – they use devices to try and manipulate their actions and thoughts. The evidence is in those C.I.A. documents, up in the District of Columbia. Worse, in the boarding schools, they took away our languages. Some Indians had unnecessary surgeries and their body parts taken away. But this tribe would have none of it. War has been declared to take down the long wires and evil machines, and the tin cans from the river."

After finishing the conversation and hanging up the phone, Marcia wondered if the killing of Presley

Whitfield and possible exoneration of Bobby Hutchings might change some things.

37.

Marcia heard that the trial was winding down and that jury would be in session, and she wanted to be there.

She got up at sunrise and put on her best summer dress: yellow sleeveless rayon that fell above her knees and waved like a flag in the wind--it was very comfortable.

She wore black leather shoes with one-inch heels and carried a mid-size brown leather bag.

She combed and pulled her hair back on both sides and pinned each side with a brown tiger-eye stone clip. She fastened a petite gold chain around her neck that had a small crucifix resting at the bottom just above the top hem of the scoop necked dress.

She arrived at court at 9:00 and walked up to Richie to see if he was okay.

The fact that she was there and cared -- buoyed his confidence. He saw her coming and smiled.

"Oh, Lord. I'm glad you're here," he said.

"Well, I wouldn't miss it. After all the work you've done, you deserve support and encouragement."

He took a deep breath and said, "Well, it should start soon. I was going to rest from my argument today, but seeing you makes a difference."

"Well, I don't understand how, but I don't have to. Just carry on with your faith of getting justice for Bobby and things will work out."

"Okay, thanks."

She turned away from him and went to find a seat among the crowd. He turned and went to his table.

Richie wasn't sure what the verdict would be. The jurors had done nothing to show him what they were thinking.

He thought about hoping for another mistrial, but the jurors would see through that and probably pronounce Bobby Hutchings guilty of second-degree murder.

But if he did get a mis-trial declared on some technicality, there would be more time to get more evidence in Bobby's favor. – including bringing Rep. Harrisen into court and finding out what connections he had with Osmond and Dr. Doebe.

But this case could go on forever, and the last thing he needed was for the jury to become frustrated with him.

Jorge had already attacked Bobby's mental health, which could give the jury some doubt about Bobby's state of mind at the time of the murder.

Richie decided to call Bobby's girlfriend, Starling Meeks, as a character witness – for insurance. She said she would be available, and she was in the courtroom.

When Starling was called to the witness stand, she arose from her seat and walked by some seated spectators and down the aisle in multi-colored ankle socks, tennis shoes, olive green army pants, and an off-white gauze top with her hair in a ponytail. She walked carefree and confident with a smile on her face as her cotton purse swung along her arm with her shoulders reared back.

After she was seated and sworn in, Richie asked her a few questions.

"How long have you known Bobby Hutchings?"

"Eight years. I met him at a wedding party," she said proudly.

"Can you describe his way of living at the time?"

Jorge objected and said the question was irrelevant to the hearing.

Judge Burrow sustained the objection.

"Okay. Starling, before Bobby found those papers in the cab, what were some of his daily activities?"

"Well. He didn't have a lot of time to do much of anything but work, since he worked at night. But when he was off, we spent time playing games, going to movies, and visiting friends, just like any other normal couple would."

"And then after the incident, what did you all do?"

"He was not so active, so we spent more time in the apartment so he wouldn't get so many headaches."

"Would you say there was a distinct difference in his behavior after he complained about someone doing something to him covertly -- when he had found blood on his pillow – and after he had visited Dr. Doebe that last time?"

"Oh, definitely. He was inattentive and confused at times. He was never like that before those incidences and when he started seeing Dr. Doebe."

"You visit Bobby regular at the jail?"

"I do. I believe in him, and it's sad this has happened. I guess he was just in the wrong place at the wrong time. But he was just trying to do right thing finding out about those papers."

"Okay. Thank you, Starling."

Jorge arose and looked straight at Starling, trying to intimidate her.

"You love Bobby right now?"

"Certainly."

"Enough to do anything for him?"

Richie let the question ride, but Starling wouldn't.

"Counselor. If you think I'm lying about what Bobby has or has not done or about his character disposition before or after May 14, you are treading on dangerous territory as a legal representative for the state by suggesting I would subvert to deceive the court with false testimony."

Jorge stopped walking back and forth. Not wanting to become embarrassed by a young girl in her working attire, he said, "I understand Miss Meeks. Thank you for your testimony and you can step down."

Richie smiled at Starling but felt sad for her – knowing this proceeding was interrupting her young life. Somehow, Richie would have to help her in the future.

Neither attorney had any more exhibits or witnesses to call.

Judge Burrow sat silently waiting for any strange interruptions or requests for additional time.

Seeing none, he asked the attorneys to give their closing statements.

38.

Jorge Melindez got up from his table and walked to the front of the courtroom near the jury box.

To gather his thoughts, he walked in a circle for a few seconds, and then he started with his closing argument, animatingly sticking his arms out and nodding his head constantly, as if that was going to make a difference.

"You have heard the evidence about the murder of Presley Whitfield. Bobby murdered him on purpose. Presley Whitfield could have been a deliveryman, visitor to one of the occupants in the building, or a neighbor just saying hello. But it didn't matter to Bobby Hutchings that day. Bobby was a paranoid individual thinking everyone was out to get him. Bobby says he saw Whitfield staring at him at Roger's Grill a few days earlier, when he went to pick up a daily fare, but staring is not a crime, and neither is walking into an apartment enclave. Yes, Whitfield had some petty theft issues in his past, but he was not a killer, and the right to self-defense has no merit for Bobby Hutchings. Plus, Hutchings has admitted to killing the man, and law enforcement has affirmed the ballistics evidence belongs to Bobby's gun. There is no other choice but to find this man guilty of murder. Our laws indicate this is a murder, and we need to be protected from such aggressors as Bobby Hutchings. Murderers are put in jail and kept there so society will be safe. To release this man from the accountability and punishment of being a murderer endangers anyone who may come in contact with him, because he thinks he is being threatened when no threat exists. For these reasons, I ask each of you on the jury to find that Bobby Hutchings is guilty of murder."

The jurors looked on as if they had just been told what to do and had no other choice, but Priscilla in the front row knew that was a lie: she had plenty of choices. She could get up and walk out of the courtroom feigning sickness, vote for the accused to be free, or not vote at all.

Richie continued to sit at his table looking through some notes, stalling for time.

Judge Burrow thought about Richie's predicament, - and just how far to go with an argument about an unseen murderer killing Presley Whitfield using Bobby Hutchings with some technology.

Finally, Richie got up and gave his final words.

"Ladies and gentlemen of the jury. We are gathered here today to judge the actions of a good man who became embroiled in a racketeering operation. He found some papers in the back of his cab - papers that contained some genetic codes and private concerns of several people. The man who lost them wanted them back, and a plan was hatched to make Bobby Hutchings be crazy, sick, or dead. None of them obviously worked. But then Presley Whitfield knew too much about this operation, and in all likelihood about the criminal organization behind it. Someone wanted him dead. And they used Bobby Hutchings by a microchip – the same one Dr. Doebe admitted to injecting into Bobby's head, to transmit voices to the head sent by a computer hereby authenticated by patent and testimony by a former computer programmer. So this is real. And that is the most important part of this trial, because there are lots of Bobby Hutchings in society who have come across illegal activities and find themselves the targets of a sophisticated technology operation to be quieted or dead."

Richie took a deep breath and walked around in a circle. He briefly looked over the spectators in the courtroom: he wanted to see their faces and how they were reacting.

"This type of event could happen to anyone in this day and age, but it is illegal. Everyone has a right to be secure in one's own person under the Constitution of the United States. When a second or multiple parties violate the privacy rights of an individual to be secure in personal thoughts, it is trespassing, coercion, and mental harassment. The evidence shows Bobby was implanted with a receiver, targeted electronically, and coerced into

249

killing Presley Whitfield. I'm asking you to find him not guilty by reason of technological coercion."

39.

Priscilla Baumgardner was skeptical. As juror
number four who had been sitting on the front row for
the week listening to the attorneys and witnesses, she
could only wonder if the trial was fabricated.

My God, she thought. *A man should have sense enough
to call the law or at least tell his harasser to get away.*

But then Priscilla grew up in a lovely home with two
educated parents that had sent her to a girls' private
school that was protected from the worst of intruders by

safety personnel. Barbed wire fencing also surrounded the compound.

Nevertheless, with her cool demeanor, the jurors looked up to her. Priscilla would make sure they could make it to the courtroom on time, back from breaks on time, and that their health needs were okay.

So it wasn't a coincidence after closing arguments had taken place that Priscilla was called on to be the mediator and spokesperson for the group.

When the group was excused to a private conference room, several differences surfaced.

One juror said, "Well, don't you all think this is all kind of crazy?"

"Crazy is normal nowadays," a young man said.

"I mean, the man hears a silent voice telling him to kill a man?"

"It is possible," the young man said.

"How do you know?"

"I was a computer information specialist, and I've seen the patents on such technology. Sometimes I think I have even heard a foreign voice."

"Well, I want to see the patents too."

Priscilla said, "Well. It's settled. Let's see the patents."

With no objections, Priscilla continued to sit in her seat.

But Bruno Harris, one of the other jurors, spoke up after a bit of time had elapsed, "You going to go and tell the bailiff Priscilla?"

"Bruno. How much is jury duty pay nowadays?"

"I don't know."

But Freda Bohart knew, "$30.00 a day, if we stay here for a while."

"Have we made a day yet?" Priscilla asked.

"Probably. We've been here three hours," Freda said.

"Thank you Freda."

The others saw the wisdom in Priscilla's thinking, so they all relaxed and thought about a free lunch and the case some more.

"Well, the guy Bobby does seem like a nice guy," Jarret Honeysuckle said.

"Nice guys do a lot of bad things," Bruno said.

Three other jurors nodded their heads in agreement.

"If I had someone breaking in my home and then advancing on me for no reason, I might pull a gun too. Presley did have a gun on him," Renee Salisbury said.

A couple jurors nodded their heads in agreement.

"How much time we got left?" another one asked.

Jordan Repass spoke up and said, "Some juries take up to a week to decide a case."

"I can't do that. I've got to baby sit tomorrow," Brenda Thornsen said.

"Okay, okay. I think the general consensus here is that Bobby, even if he wasn't coerced somehow into killing the guy, he had reason. The victim was a criminal for one thing," Priscilla said.

"Yeah. We all agree," Brenda said. "Let's get on with it."

"No. I want to see the patents," Bruno said.

"Okay. I'll tell the bailiff," said Priscilla.

Priscilla got up with her purse strings attached to one arm and walked over to the door and knocked on it.

The bailiff opened the door slowly and Priscilla motioned him to the side and said, "We want to see the patents for the mind control technology."

The bailiff nodded his head. He walked over to the judge's podium and told the judge.

Judge Burrow did not look surprised. He nodded for the bailiff to go over to Richie and get them.

The bailiff walked over to Richie and asked for the patents.

Richie looked up in surprise; then a big smile came across his face and he almost dropped a stack of papers on the floor trying to find the patent listings and descriptions of the media involved.

Once he found three different pages of three different patents that had been registered with the Patent Office, he gave them to the bailiff. The bailiff went to the conference room and opened the door; he gave the papers to Priscilla.

The patent papers were passed around the room, with each juror taking a minute to look over the jargon descriptions and applications of the media – and the procedures used for influencing someone with energy fields.

Each juror looked stone-faced after looking at the papers for a minute or two, and the papers finally ended up back at Priscilla.

"Satisfied?"

No one objected.

"That takes care of this one charge that he's not guilty of malicious murder. What about this pre-meditation thing?"

Repass spoke up and said, "Naw. He had no idea Presley was coming to harass him. He just had a gun to protect himself. I think Bobby was defending himself."

Several other jurors nodded their heads. One said, "Right."

After a few seconds, Priscilla said, "Okay, case closed, and it has been nice meeting you all."

"What are you going to do Priscilla?" Brenda asked.

"I'm going to knock on that door over there and tell the bailiff we've reached a decision, and then I'm going out to read the charges on this note and tell everyone within hearing range that Bobby Hutchings is not guilty. And then I'm walking out of this courthouse and visiting the nearest pub to have a drink."

"You don't mean alcohol, do you Priscilla?" Bruno said.

"That and more if I can get it."

"Hey. Can I go too?" Rusty Argonne asked.

"We're all going to the pub. Drinks are on Mr. Dudley over there since he can afford to wear linen pants, silk shirts, and gold links everyday he comes to trial."

Dudley just smiled and didn't say a word; he nodded his head as a shameful boy would.

The jurors quieted themselves, waiting for Priscilla to lead them on, but Priscilla sat, as if waiting for a chorus to sing.

No song played but the group CARES outside the courthouse began shouting, "Justice for Bobby Hutchings".

To which Dudley responded, "It's time to go."

40.

The jury walked back to their seats and sat down while Priscilla made sure they were all behaving and not giving away the verdict before she was asked to read it aloud: she didn't want anything to mess up her appointment to celebrate the end of this madness.

With all her companions looking fit and relaxed, and the courtroom silent as a virgin forest with no people in it, the judge asked her if the jury had reached a verdict.

"We have, Your Honor," she said.

Then she waited for him in anticipation while looking at the gawking eyes of the attorneys and spectators in the courtroom.

For once in my life, I am the center of attention, she thought. *I kind of like this. Maybe we should have waited another day.*

Meanwhile, the protesters outside continued their shouting: "Justice for Bobby Hutchings".

"Well. What is it lady?" the Judge asked.

Priscilla looked down at the notepaper slowly, all the time soaking in the spotlight of being on a stage, and she smiled. Judge Burrow could see what was happening and just bowed and shook his head.

"We the jury, find the defendant Bobby Hutchings on the first charge of pre-meditated murder: not guilty. On the second charge of murdering with malicious and malcontent, we find the defendant Bobby Hutchings not guilty."

An "ooh" and "ah" reverberated throughout the courtroom, with a few members of the CARES group smiling and hugging each other.

Judge Burrow re-iterated Priscilla's statements, thanked the jury for their service, and said they were free to go. He said Bobby Hutchings was free to go, tapped his gavel to the podium, and said, "This trial is over."

Jorge looked on astonishment, still wondering if what he had just heard was right. His associate confirmed that he did and wondered out loud about an appeal.

Jorge shook his head and said, "Oh, this is not over yet. It's like a game in the first quarter and there are three more to play."

Richie Granger knew there could be more to this trial than what had just happened.

Dr. Doebe, though he was granted immunity from prosecution, would still be liable for a malpractice lawsuit: it was the only way to get redemption for Bobby Hutchings.

But first, Richie and company would celebrate. He would tell the Indian group that one of their own was vindicated, and that if the decision was termed "precedential"; many other innocent Indian victims of mind control technology could be freed.

Marcia was happy. She immediately went to Richie and gave him a big hug. She told him how proud she was of him.

A celebration was in order, but only if Jim Cloudwaters, Emma, and the CARES group could come and be a part of it.

It was the least Marcia could do for a group who had been oppressed for centuries.

****

I hope you have enjoyed this book. I try to write books to be entertaining – and informative.

I'm sure are grammar mistakes in this book. I don't have a team of editors, proofreaders, and reviewers, probably because I speak the truth about matters and the establishment does not want my books printed.

Though this book is fiction, there is truth and personal experience behind the writing.

And yes, I am a victim of persecution.

But I trudge on and hope to provide some knowledge that will put the persecutors away.

If you are targeted, micro-chipped, and or persecuted, I certainly hope you become free of such oppression.

One action that can help, is bowing to a holy God and accepting Jesus Christ as Savior.

And then you can begin the fight to help others.

Kenneth M. Lee, Christmas, 2022

www.ingramcontent.com/pod-product-compliance
Lightning Source LLC
Chambersburg PA
CBHW050110280326
41933CB00010B/1042